Education by
Design

A Guide to Technology Across the Curriculum

Tristram Shepard

Stanley Thornes (Publishers) Ltd

First published in 1990 by:
Stanley Thornes (Publishers) Ltd
Old Station Drive
Leckhampton
Cheltenham GL53 0DN
England

British Library Cataloguing in Publication Data
Shepard, Tristram
  Education by design: a guide to technology across the curriculum.
  1. Schools. Curriculum subjects: Crafts, design &
  technology
  I. Title
  607.1

  ISBN 0-7487-0218-0

Typeset in 10/11pt Rockwell
Printed and Bound in Great Britain by Ebenezer Baylis & Son, Worcester.

Education by
Design

For my Mother, Father and Grandmother

Acknowledgements

I would particularly like to thank the following individuals who, during our various conversations and collaborations over the past ten years, have helped me to shape the thoughts and actions which have enabled me to write both *Introducing Design* and *Education by Design*:

Eileen Adams, Ken Baynes, Krysia Brochocka, Martyn Dukes, Gill Kendall, Richard Kimbell, Brian Hurlow, Bill Lazard, Loraine Moore, David Neeves, Philip Poole, Evie Safarewicz and Stephen Scoffham.

I must also acknowledge the considerable influence of Nigel Cross and David Walker of the Design Discipline of The Open University through the publications produced under their chairmanship of courses T262 (Man-made Futures) and T263 (Design: Products and Processes).

I am also grateful to Philip Poole for reading and commenting on the text, to Pat Rowlinson, formerly of Hutchinson Education, who made both publications possible in the first place, and to Tristram Ariss for his imaginative, patient and persistent design.

Tristram Shepard
Canterbury, July 1989

If you would like to receive information about current and forthcoming publications for Design and Technology from Stanley Thornes, please write to:

Design and Technology Publisher
Stanley Thornes (Publishers) Ltd
Old Station Drive
Leckhampton
Cheltenham
GL53 0DN

Contents

Introduction

From *Design Strategies*, Chris Jones, TV Broadcast Notes, T262 Man-made Futures, The Open University, 1976

The difficulty with academic, book learning is that it tends to make you think that if something's not in a book, then it's not right. In design, it's almost the opposite: it's only really right if it's out there, in actual life.

The past

During 1987 the Government announced that, as part of their proposed National Curriculum, all pupils from 5 to 16 would be expected to study something called **technology**. In the same year the MSC made it clear to schools applying for funding through its TVEI extension programme that a commitment to **technology for all** was obligatory. As a consequence, during 1988, many local authority advisers, headteachers, TVEI co-ordinators and classroom teachers began to start asking:

- What is technological education?
- How can it be delivered within the curriculum?
- To what extent is it being provided already?

The answers they often found to their questions were that:

- there was no simple definition or explanation of what technological education was or might be
- there was little in the way of tried and tested ways of delivering it
- to a certain extent it was already being provided in many subjects and schools, but lacked effective co-ordination.

By the end of 1988, **technology** had become **design and technology**, and the National Curriculum Working Party had published their Interim Report, setting out the general direction of the development and levels of attainment which were likely to be expected. Their final Consultative Report, which contained detailed attainment targets and programmes of study, appeared in June 1989.

This was a time of much debate and considerable confusion as to the future of design and technological education. Many teachers initially assumed that 'technology' would be all about electronics, computers and other sophisticated machines and devices. The use of the term 'design and make' was frequently equated with constructing three-dimensional wood, metal and plastic products, which made the cross-curricular dimensions difficult to identify. Multi-disciplinary work was initially identified as 'good practice', even when it was neither truly cross-curricular, nor involved developmental, speculative design and technological activity. Some schools rushed to carve design and technology up into discrete subject areas, without understanding the pupil-centred approach which is really needed if it is to be effectively delivered.

The present

Although the intellectual ideas behind a broad approach to design and technological education are by no means new, their proposed implementation on a large scale represents one of the most fundamental changes required by the National Curriculum. At its heart lies the need to adopt new approaches to the processes of teaching and learning at secondary level, without which it is unlikely that the high demands of the levels of attainment will be reached. The National Curriculum is not a rigid prescription, and it will only come to be effectively delivered when inspired, experienced and confident teachers are able to bring the aims and processes of design and technological education to life in the classroom.

The various documents which set out the requirements for design and technology in the National Curriculum and TVEI take a considerable time to read, unravel, understand and begin to translate into classroom terms. Close examination reveals many implications and issues which need to be recognised and discussed before planning, commencing and developing implementation in schools: whilst presenting an exciting and challenging vision of the future, there is little in the way of guidance as to shorter-term strategies for delivery.

Education by Design: a Guide to Technology Across the Curriculum is therefore intended to help clarify and identify some (but by no means all) of the most immediate issues involved. It also presents and explains the particular philosophy, methodology and practice on which *Introducing Design: Technology Across the Curriculum* was based, and to examine the ways it can be used in the classroom to help meet the requirements of the National Curriculum and TVEI. As such it is therefore mostly an account of one possible approach and vision, and you may well find yourself agreeing or disagreeing with different sections of the book, or feeling that things would need to be done in a slightly different way in your school. Whatever your own opinions are, however, you will have been introduced to many of the important issues which are at the heart of the implementation of the proposed National Curriculum and TVEI initiatives. You will also have increased your awareness of the possibly very different perceptions and ideas of your colleagues: teamwork is an essential ingredient to success in establishing the most appropriate approaches and methods of delivery for your school.

The future?

Before you start you will need to be fully aware that implementing design and technology is going to require a fundamental re-appraisal of:

- your own awareness and understanding about what design and technological education is, or might be
- the material you present in the classroom and the way in which you present it
- the academic, intellectual and utilitarian curriculum and staffing policies of your school as a whole.

Design and technology in the National Curriculum involves a great deal more than girls doing woodwork and metalwork and boys doing cookery and learning how to sew. A single department, or even a number of departments working separately, are unlikely to be able to deliver the programmes of study effectively. In future, teachers of art and design, CDT, home economics, business studies and information technology are going to need to start to work very much more closely together: the importance of their successful amalgamation into something new called 'design and technology' cannot be stressed enough. Discrete module or 'circus' based courses centred on specific materials or technologies (e.g. plastics or electronics) are unlikely to be effective because the final attainment targets necessitate a broad approach in which all the parts are interconnected through a series of design tasks. Although some short-term assignments might be based on improving specific design skills or introducing new technologies, teachers will, over a period of time, need to be encouraged to let go of their previous responsibility to deliver a specialised discrete subject area: it is not a matter of simply carving up the programmes of study to identify which bit art and design will cover, which section IT will deal with and so on. Instead it is eventually expected that common starting points ('contexts') will be agreed and pupils invited to identify a wide range of appropriate tasks. Each teacher therefore needs to identify the contribution he or she will be able to make as a member of a team when pupils need to have access to particular areas of expertise.

All this represents a very considerable challenge to the individual classroom teacher, to the management teams of each school, and to the providers of in-service training. Working through this book is not going to transform anyone immediately into a successful teacher of design and technology – a great deal of further guidance and direct experience of managing appropriate activities in the classroom will also be necessary.

It is likely to be some time before tried and tested 'ready-to-wear' packages of INSET and classroom material appear on the shelves, or any nationally accepted 'brand-leaders' begin to emerge. So the first steps need to be for each teacher to understand more about what design and technology really is, and to identify the extent to which it is being provided already. Only then can the process of development begin, and it will certainly be one which requires much imagination, experimentation, evaluation, planning, patience and persistence to ensure that we avoid the construction of quick-build, low-cost, high-rise curriculum structures that no-one wants to teach or learn in.

From *Beyond Design Education*, Ken Baynes, article in Journal of Art and Design Education, Vol 1 No1 1982, NSEAD, Carfax Publishing

I do not believe that the creation of visual literacy or design awareness is something that will yield to any grand curriculum strategy. It is a matter of footwork. It is a matter of the 'small print' of teaching. It is to do with building up confidence. It is about people meeting to change one another and to create something new. At national level it means encouraging diversity and unique local initiatives. It means putting people in touch with one another and leaving them to get on with it.

What to expect

In *Education By Design: a Guide to Technology Across the Curriculum*, the first session encourages thought about our present expectations of what the words **technology**, **design** and a third, closely related word, **creativity** generally refer to: the common stereotyped images we tend to have of them are frequently misleading and unhelpful. The second session describes design, technology and creativity within the **World of Education**. It begins with an account of the historical evolution of the intellectual ideas which lie behind design and technological education, making selected reference to the works of a wide range of philosophers, pioneers, visionary educationalists and writers, thus providing a valuable bibliography for further reference. Placed in their educational context, the worlds of design, technology and creativity reveal their potential as vehicles for learning.

The third session is intended to clarify the National Curriculum proposals and raise some of the important practical issues involved in planning and structuring effective design and technological activity. The idea of a 'context', and the differences between 'artefacts, systems and environments' are explained. The particular difficulties likely to be faced in implementing cross-curricular programmes are examined in terms of individual teaching styles and the need to 'de-sign' the curriculum. Approaches to the monitoring and assessment of work are also discussed.

The fourth session describes the important process-based 'design skills' in considerably more detail, providing a general indication of the comparative levels of achievement which pupils might be expected to be attain. The fifth and final session includes detailed notes on most of the assignments in *Introducing Design* to assist delivery and suggest further sources of information.

The material is presented in a similar way to familiar GCSE training manuals, providing discussion material and short-term activities for cross-curricular INSET meetings. Each session invites participants to analyse and evaluate their present practice and circumstances, and to speculate on possible new strategies which could be adopted. There is no prescribed time allocation for each session or activity, but it could be anticipated that to read and discuss the first three sessions adequately in a group would take at least two days. Alternatively, of course, the guide can be just as effectively read by the individual.

This publication is intended for use by teachers, school senior-management teams, heads of faculties, departments and new subject-clusters, technology co-ordinators, and other providers of cross-curricular design and technology INSET. Parallel reference to the reports and requirements of TVEI and the National Curriculum is advised. Book references which appear in the left hand column of each page have been included as particular recommendation for further reading by teachers and providers of INSET. In the fourth session, the page numbers refer to *Introducing Design*.

Forms for use in relation to projects follow the final session and may be photocopied free of charge if wished provided the source acknowledgement at the bottom is not deleted.

SESSION 1   Technology, design and creativity

The world of technology

Book references which appear in the left-hand column of each page have been included as particular recommendation for further reading by teachers and providers of INSET.

Designing the Future Unit 1, Man-made Futures (T262)
Cross, Elliot and Roy
Open University Publications, 1975

It is common practice to begin by providing a series of definitions of 'design' and 'technology', but to do so can be to impose limitations and boundaries on concepts which are open-ended, all-embracing and constantly changing. It is perhaps more useful to talk about our **impressions** or the common **images** we have of **technology**, **design**, and a third closely-related and often much misunderstood word, **creativity**. In this way it becomes possible to begin to identify some of the considerable pre-conceptions we all have about them, and which cloud our visions of their real meaning.

Images of technology

What does the word 'technology' mean to you? Without attempting any definitions, or thinking about its educational context, make a note of the first few visual images which come to mind.

Living with Technology
Introduction: Technology and Human Values (T101)
Naughton, J
The Open University, 1979

Technology Today
de Bono, E (Ed)
Routledge & Kegan Paul, 1971

Future Shock
Toffler, A
Bodley Head, 1970

Design for the Real World
Papanek, V
Thames and Hudson, 1972

Compare what you have written with others in your group. You may be surprised at the range and type of responses everyone has made. To many people the word 'technology' initially seems to conjure up images of things like:

- large chemical plants and power-stations
- men (and specifically men) in white coats in laboratories, and in yellow hats on building sites
- micro-chips, laser-beams, fibre-optics and telecommunication systems
- getting to the moon, and star-wars
- mechanical reproduction of things made mainly from metals and plastics
- polluted rivers and damaged ozone layers.

These are what are often termed 'high' technology images. Many of us feel a little in awe of the cleverness of the highly trained specialists who manipulate and control these things we have come to depend on, but don't really understand.

Maybe though, your lists included some rather different sorts of images:

- the chair you are sitting on
- the room you are in at present
- the clothes you are wearing
- the book you are now reading
- the meal you will prepare this evening
- the programmes you watch on television.

All these rather more familiar images are technological as well: we all use a wide range of common materials, machines, devices, environments and communication systems everyday without thinking very much about it. Most of these we feel much less threatened by – many we can create or maintain ourselves, or know that they can be easily made or mended by almost anyone. At the most basic level, however, technology is really about something even more fundamental – our day-to-day survival. What technology actually does is to help people to survive more effectively and comfortably.

If you haven't already done so, you should now read the passage on page 5 of *Introducing Design: Technology Across the Curriculum* headed 'Technology and us'. Make a list of some of the everyday things you possess which help extend the capability of your body, brain and/or senses.

Survival by technology

Our most essential survival needs are physiological – food, water, warmth and air – which are provided for by the things we eat and drink, our clothing, and a shelter of some sort. These are followed by safety needs – to feel free from threat in any aspect of our survival. Finally we all want to feel that we belong somewhere – a sense of community, and that someone loves and cares for us. Work enables us to feel that we are worthwhile and capable, and are valued by the society we live in. We need to be able to rest, relax and play, to be healthy, to be able to develop our capabilities and to achieve periods of joy, happiness and tranquillity. To facilitate and enhance our achievement of these things, some form of transport is often needed, together with communication systems and a range of everyday objects.

We also seem to need a sense of purpose and direction, of anticipated change for the better – an optimistic vision of the future. It is technology that we frequently look towards to bring about such changes. These survival needs are of fundamental concern to us all, and, consciously or unconsciously, they have a profound effect on every action we take.

Attitudes towards technology

Different people have different opinions about technology. For example, do you think technology is generally good or bad? Do the advantages outweigh the disadvantages? Is it the key to our future survival or to our destruction?

Consider the following statements and tick or cross the ones which you feel you agree or disagree with the most:
☐ Without technology we would be unable to survive, and with further progress we will be able to solve all the problems in the world.
☐ Technological development is a great challenge, worthwhile for its own sake.
☐ Advanced technological projects generate economic growth and hence higher living standards.
☐ Technological achievements considerably enhance the prestige of the nation.
☐ We clearly need technological devices and systems, but do they really need to be as sophisticated as they are?
☐ Greater controls on the use of technology are urgently needed to prevent environmental damage.
☐ More attention should be paid to the immediate, basic survival needs of the homeless and starving.
☐ Decisions about technological change should not be left to the 'experts'.

Discuss your responses with the rest of your group – but make sure you set a clear time limit, as these are very emotive issues. There are of course no right or wrong answers to these questions, but they should help you to become more aware of:
● your own feeling about technology
● the wide range of opinions which other people have.

You may discover that you, or others in the group, are clear pro- or anti-technologists. Or perhaps there will be a more balanced view that we have to accept that technology is here to stay and will keep advancing and changing our lives. If we ignore it or condemn it out of hand it will not go away. But we must also have to accept that everything is part of a larger system, and a system operates effectively in a state of balance. Systems can and do change, but only slowly, so that any imbalance in one part can be stabilised by other parts. We need to tread carefully if we are to continue to survive.

As teachers it is important to be aware of our own personal attitudes towards technology, and to appreciate the views of others. The further educational relevance of our images of technology, our attitudes towards it and the way it enhances our survival will be explored and discussed in a later session.

The world of design

Images of design

Conran Directory of Design
Bayley, S (Ed)
Conran Octopus, 1985

As with technology, it can be a mistake to try and rigidly define the word 'design', because we use it in so many different situations to mean different things. It is, however, helpful to be aware that it can be

a noun – referring to an existing artefact, or

a verb – the process of designing something.

Design is a very fashionable word at present. Note down the first images which occur to you on hearing the word 'design'.

The Nature and Aesthetics of Design
Pye, D
Barrie and Jenkins Ltd, 1978

What is a Designer?
Potter, N
Hyphen Press, 1980

Design magazine
Design Council Publications
(monthly)

Compare your responses with those of the rest of your group. Some current stereotype images are along the lines of:

- smartly dressed young men and women guesting on chat shows, talking about their latest cars or clothes which few of us could afford to buy
- a new kitchen with a complete set of matching cupboards, curtains, cutlery, etc.
- a smart matt-black corkscrew which looks really good, but you can't actually get to work
- the colourful logo which appears at the top of an estate agent's letterhead.

What all these products, places and communications have in common is that they are very clearly intended to look first and foremost as if their appearance has been uniquely 'designed' by someone. It all seems to be about clever marketing, corporate images and super-slick stylish packaging of things everyone thinks he or she wants, but no one really needs. These days businesses have realised that design helps sell their products.

Think of an object you have at home which you would describe as an example of good design. Explain to the rest of your group why you chose it.

Again, you might be surprised at the wide variety of objects chosen, and the range of reasons given to justify its selection:

- It works well and has passed the test of time.
- It looks good on the sideboard.
- It was excellent value for money.
- I enjoy using it.

Of course there is also the image of today's modern professional 'designer' – no longer a 'commercial artist', but young, upwardly mobile, magic-marker at the ready, creative, but thanks to the evolution of the personal organiser, well in control. To be a designer is to be at the cutting edge of today's lifestyle. These days everyone wants to be a designer.

Do you know anyone who is a professional designer – an architect, engineer or graphic or interior designer perhaps? Discuss the extent to which he or she conforms to our stereotype images.

Attitudes towards design

By now a range of attitudes towards the value of design will probably have begun to emerge. In your group discuss the accuracy of the following statements:

- Good design is about form following function.
- Design is 'icing on the cake' – making things look nice.
- Design is a phoney way of persuading you to buy things which fall apart soon after you've got them, so you have to buy another.

Then discuss the particular qualities you think might make someone a successful designer:

- good at drawing?
- imaginative?
- strong business sense?
- ability to work well with his or her hands?
- convincing salesperson?

Again, there are no right or wrong answers or opinions: these activities have not been meant to demonstrate that design and designers are good or bad, profitable or wasteful, sincere or confidence-tricksters. Instead they should have raised your awareness of the range of images and opinions frequently perceived and expressed by the general public.

You may already feel yourself to be particularly well informed about what professional design is, might or should be, but if not, the following section is intended to serve as a brief introduction.

Industry and commerce by design

People have been designing and making products, places and communications for thousands of years, but it was only during the Industrial Revolution that the term 'design' was used to describe a 'plan', originated by one person, for someone else to make.

Today, professional designers tend to work in various specialised disciplines. Some are primarily concerned with three-dimensional work, such as transport, product, furniture or interior design. Others work in fashion and fabrics, graphics, or as architects. Town-planners and engineers are designers too. Most of them are involved with the creation and specification of designs for the mass production of everyday products, places and communications we take for granted, although some work on a smaller scale for batch, or one-off production of very high quality. All designers are basically problem-finders and solvers, responsible for presenting technological capability in forms which are physically and emotionally acceptable to people, within the restraints of safety and financial viability.

Well-designed products, places and communications are becoming seen as essential to success and survival in the market-place, and so the training of future designers has come to be recognised as a priority area in further education. Each professional discipline has become highly specialised, requiring its own particular mix of knowledge, skills and experience, and there is a wide range of degree courses in the United Kingdom producing graduates of such high calibre that they are sought the world over. Most of the courses in graphic, fashion and 3D design are within polytechnics in faculties of art and design – often former colleges of art, and are thus rooted in the visual studies of the fine arts. There are separate university, polytechnic and college degree courses in architecture, town planning and engineering. All these courses tend to be vocationally rather than academically orientated and commercial practices and real-world problems dominate content.

In terms of secondary education, as we shall discuss in more detail in the next session, many of the practical activities which are appropriate to the delivery of design and technological education are based on the practice of professional designers in a wide variety of disciplines.

The world of creativity

Creative Visualisation
Shone, R
Thorsons, 1984

Images of creativity

Again, like the words 'design' and 'technology', creativity suggests different things to different people in different situations.

What are the popular images and misconceptions of creativity? Make a note of the first thoughts you have about something or someone described as creative.

Creativity and Industry
Whitfield, P R
Penguin, 1975

The Keys to Creativity
Evans and Deehan
Grafton, 1988

de Bono's Thinking Course
de Bono, E
BBC Publications, 1982

Compare your response with others in the group. A common image is perhaps that of the mad scientist, shabbily dressed, late for appointments, generally unreliable, forgetful, obsessed with his (yes, *his*) research, living in a world of his own. Or maybe of the great artist, poet or composer – manic-depressive, eccentric, irresponsible, sensitive, probably alcoholic. The lifestyle of creative people is different: they don't work regular hours, and they are supposed to be less concerned with earning and looking after money, as they value their work more. We also tend to believe that such people have special mystical gifts and talents which make them somehow different from the rest of us. Many people who consider themselves non-creative feel they would like to be more individual and spontaneous and so have a more satisfying life; as a consequence they tend to feel a little envious of those who are.

In reality, however, everybody to a greater or lesser extent has the basic ability to be creative. It is far from a special gift of the select few, but is a capability we all share – something we can learn, or to be more accurate, re-learn, to do. Much depends on the way our individual personalities, formed during childhood, enable us to replace freely old perceptions with new ones, or to combine old ideas in new ways – and we don't have to be mixing chemicals or paint when we do so.

Do you consider yourself to be creative? Write down the things you do as a teacher which you think could be described as creative, and any things which you do outside your job.

Compare your notes with the rest of the group. Again you should not be surprised to find a wide range of activities which have been identified, and a variety of situations in which they seem to occur. Maybe you thought of some of the following examples:
- directing the school play
- persuading colleagues to adopt fresh approaches
- seeing a new way of explaining something to pupils
- adapting a recipe
- going on holiday somewhere you have never been before.

Although much remains undiscovered, over the past fifty or so years psychologists have come to understand a great deal more about the mental processes of creativity in everyday thinking. They tend to describe four common stages: preparation, incubation, illumination and verification. Important discoveries have also been made about the differences between the functions and activities of the left and right hemispheres of the brain. The left side seems to control rational, analytic thinking, language skills, mathematical functions and sequentially ordered thinking. The right brain controls intuitive functions, spatial orientation, spatial constructions, crafts, skills, art, music, creative expression, and emotional responses. Many of us have simply never developed our abilities equally.

The term 'creative visualisation' describes the use of the heightened imagination of positive visual images to increase performance in sport and management, and to accelerate recovery from physical and mental illness. Psychologists also refer to the 'peak experience' which seems to provide us with the motivation for much creative activity. You may be more familiar with the terms 'lateral' and 'divergent' thinking which are often associated with creative thinking. Whilst they contribute to creativity, they only form part of the skills which are needed.

Recognising creative thinking

The following attitudes and activities seem to be amongst those which contribute to creative thinking, and have been observed in many people, whatever their profession. Place a tick by those which seem to best describe the way you think:

- ☐ a willingness to suspend judgement about things – to accept that other interpretations and outcomes might be possible
- ☐ seeing connections between things which are not normally related
- ☐ being open to new ideas, new attitudes, new ways of doing things
- ☐ having a willingness to take mental or physical risks within certain safety limits
- ☐ lessening inhibitions with regard to the expression of emotions and subjective personal opinions
- ☐ having faith in intuitive, spontaneous or outlandish responses
- ☐ not being afraid of being wrong or unconventional
- ☐ a willingness to play like a child – to enjoy experimenting with ideas, images, materials, structures, etc
- ☐ feeling free to fantasise
- ☐ not feeling threatened by paradoxes, ambiguities, contradictions and things which cannot be rationally explained
- ☐ being willing to abandon promising ideas in the interests of conciseness
- ☐ patience, persistence, determination.

By this point you may be realising you probably have a much greater potential to be creative than you originally thought. Or, if you already feel yourself to be creative, perhaps you are beginning to understand more about why you think the way you do. It is necessary to understand and recognise the processes in action if you are to develop the creative abilities of your pupils, and to become more aware of the wide range of attitudes which seem to be involved in thinking more creatively.

SESSION 2 The world of education

In the previous session we examined the three worlds of technology, design and creativity, and discovered that we all share many misconceptions about them. There is clearly a great deal of overlap between them, yet oddly enough the three worlds seem to exist more or less separately.

This session is about a fourth world, that of **education**, which **we** all inhabit. This too is full of misconceptions and unnecessary separations. It is a world of brave new initiatives and radical reforms which often prove to be no more than old ideas repackaged and freshly labelled, and of acronyms, buzz-words and phrases which mean different things to different people (or frequently nothing at all!). If we are to make realistic progress we need to stop working at cross-purposes and make an effort to clarify and agree on what we mean and what we are trying to achieve.

Education evolving by design

In terms of its practical and co-ordinated implementation, design and technological education will be an innovation, but the concepts which lie behind it are, however, by no means new. The current proposals for a broad, cross-curricular approach are firmly rooted in a series of theories, philosophies, methodologies and visions, some of which have been around for centuries.

This section is intended to provide a brief overview of the richness of thought and debate which has brought us to this point in the development and implementation of design and technology in schools. It is an introductory, and highly selective, further reading guide to some of the leading thinkers and writers: for purposes of brevity, many of the explanations of the underlying theories and recommendations have been considerably simplified.

First thoughts

The Three Rs
Archer, B
Design Studies Vol 1, No 1
Butterworth and Co, July 1979

Education since 1800
Morrish, I
George Allen and Unwin, 1970

How We Think
Dewey, J
Harrap, 1910

Experience and Education
Dewey, J
Collier-Macmillan, 1979
(first published 1938)

The Play Way
Cook, C
Heinemann, 1917

The Aims of Education and Other Essays
Whitehead, A N
Williams and Norgate, 1929
(re-printed by Benn, 1973)

The Process of Education
Bruner, J
Oxford University Press, 1961

The works of the great philosophers seem to be a popular starting point for many design educationalists. Plato, for example, discusses the relationship between the awareness of goodness of form in the applied arts and good character and discipline in people. Francis Bacon (the playwright, not the painter) proclaimed nearly 400 years ago in *To the King* that the four attributes of intelligence were to be able to invent, judge, retain and deliver. Meanwhile it has been suggested that before the demise of the craft guilds and the dominance of the universities, the original eighteenth century version of the '3Rs' was in fact 'Reading and writing, Reckoning and figuring, and Wroughting and wrighting (wroughting meaning knowing how things are brought about, and wrighting, how to act in order to bring them about).

At the turn of the nineteenth century the philosopher, psychologist and educator, J F Herbart, identified the 'five formal steps' of problem-solving as 'preparation, presentation, association, generalisation and application', paralleled in John Dewey's *Problem Method* of 1910 which described the stages of progress as:
* confusion, doubt and perplexity owing to the fact that the nature and significance of the problem-situation has not yet been ascertained
* conjecture, in which the problem-solver attempts a tentative interpretation of the given information, based on general knowledge of familiar patterns of behaviour
* examination, exploration, survey and analysis to clarify and define further the problem under consideration
* elaboration of the hypothesis in order to make it more precise and consistent as it begins to square with a wider range of available elements and data
* validation (testing) of the hypothesis as an organised plan of action to be applied to the existing state of affairs.

In the context of classroom activity Dewey makes a number of important observations in terms of the experiences of the pupil:

- The problem must be a real one, that is, real to the pupil, and be a stimulus to further thought.
- The pupil must have the necessary information, and make the observations required to deal with the problem.
- The pupil needs to be placed in the position of the researcher, developing his or her ideas and seeking an individual solution.
- The pupil must be allowed to try out and test the validity of his or her own conclusions.

Dewey was particularly concerned with the processes involved in the basic human activity of survival; satisfying our needs for food, clothing and reasonable comfort. It is these basic survival needs which are real to children. Through this he evolved a concept we know today as 'child-centred learning', stressing the need to place the problem in a situation which is real to the pupil. Taking this idea further, Caldwell Cook's *The Play Way*, popular in the 1950s, but written in 1917, includes a 'desert island' activity, rather proving the saying that there is 'nothing new under the sun'. In 1932 A N Whitehead talked of the 'three main roads' of:

the way of literary culture, the way of scientific culture, and the way of technical culture. No one of these methods can be exclusively followed without grave loss of intellectual activity and of character.

During the 1960s the major impetus for 'process-based learning' can be traced to J S Bruner's *The Process of Education*. His (pre-equal opportunities entitled) *Man: a Course of Study* (MACOS) programme of 1965 brought together an inter-disciplinary team to use the exploration of the evolution of human-beings as a species, based on the 'five great humanising forces': tool-making, language, social organisation, the management of childhood, and man's urge to explain.

Design education: The state-of-the-art

Design Education: Problem-Solving and Visual Experience
Green, P
Batsford, 1974

About Design
Baynes, K
Design Council Publications, 1976

Design Education in Schools
Alward, B (Ed)
Evans, 1973

Design in General Education
(Report)
Royal College of Art, 1976

Design in General Education
Harahan, J (Ed)
The Design Council, 1978

Designerly Ways of Knowing
Cross, Cross and Glyn,
The Open University, 1986

Technology in Schools
Cross and McCormick (Eds)
The Open University, 1986

Design Education at Secondary Level
Design Council, 1980

Design and Primary Education
Design Council, 1987

Something called 'design education' began to emerge during the late 1960s, pioneered by Hornsey College of Art's teacher education course which began to identify the educational potential and value of a broad, cross-curricular approach to design and designing. Peter Green's *Design Education: Problem-solving and Visual Experience* publication of 1974 remains an extraordinary blueprint and is remarkable in its vision of a multi-disciplinary approach. Leicestershire initiated an innovative programme in its new upper-schools, and an A level in Design was launched by the Oxford Delegacy of Local Examinations. The National Association of Design Education was formed, and the Schools Council Design and Craft Project established at Keele University.

During the 1970s and early 1980s the focus shifted to the Design Education Unit of the Royal College of Art, with the publication of their report *Design in General Education* which presented the case for design as the third dimension of the curriculum, and the Art and the Built Environment Working Parties Project.

Meanwhile the significance of the contribution of the emerging 'design discipline' of the Faculty of Technology of the Open University during the 1970s cannot be ignored. Its more recent work in design and technological education represents the current frontier of research into the basis of designerly 'ways of knowing' in an educational context. The DES outlined a cross-curricular approach to technology in the 1977 HMI *Curriculum 11-16*, and the Design Council's 1980 publication *Design in Secondary Education Report* remains remarkably visionary in its recommendations, now more than equally supported by their 1986 *Design in Primary Education Report*.

The Design and Technology Assessment of Performance Unit was established in the early 1980s, and in 1985, based at Goldsmith's College, began to prepare for its 1988 survey of the current design and technological capabilities of 15 year-olds. Its *Framework for Assessment* report of 1987 provides probably the most concise description to date of the processes of design and places them in an broad curricular context. Geoffrey Harrison and Paul Black's Nottingham Technology Project reported in 1988 indicating the potential, and some of the possible difficulties, of implementing cross-curricular work.

Second thoughts

There are many other outstanding philosophers, pioneers, visionaries, educationalists and writers – Froebel, Rousseau, Montessori, and Steiner, for example, – whose work is highly relevant to current ideas about design and technological education. There are many other official reports and documents – by Crowther (1959), and Dainton (1968), for example – which were remarkably enlightened in their findings. Unfortunately none of their ideas have ever been implemented on a large enough scale to have had a lasting and fundamental effect on the educational system. The recommendations and requirements of the National Curriculum, however, now appear to provide the potential opportunity to do so in a co-ordinated and structured way.

So design and technological education as a concept already has a well-established philosophy and research-base, albeit unco-ordinated: what is new is its proposed implementation in schools right across the country. There is still, however, a great deal of further research and curriculum development work to be done before coherent, tried and tested, structured delivery strategies for teachers and pupils become available.

What information and published material on design and technological education currently exists in your school? Some departments, particularly CDT, home economics, and art and design may well have some of the reports and books referred to above. Individual staff may already be informed as to the ideas of particular theorists, or be aware of other relevant publications and curriculum development projects not mentioned here.

Technological education

In the previous session, 'The World of Technology', it was suggested that the visions we have of technology tend to relate to sophisticated and highly specialised concepts, rather than to the provision of our basic survival needs.

In Place of Confusion: Technology and Science in the School Curriculum
Harrison and Black
National Centre for School Technology
Nottingham, 1985

In 1985 Geoffrey Harrison and Paul Black's *In Place of Confusion* identified three complementary sets of **educational aims** for technology:
- to give children an **awareness** of technology, and its implications as a resource for the achievement of human purpose
- to develop **practical capability** to engage in technological activities
- to help children acquire the **resources** of knowledge and intellectual and physical skills.

They proceed to discuss a diverse range of activities, from creating a self-propelled flying machine to composing a piece of music or a painting, decorating a living room and managing a small business, which can contribute to the development of human capability through the application of a common range of 'action-based qualities and the resources of knowledge, skill and experience.'

Viewed in this way, many of the current applied science or CDT-based 'Project Technology' approaches, which often centre on a specific knowledge-base and range of construction skills relating to topics such as electronics, mechanics and energy systems, make an often limited contribution towards the development of an understanding of the way in which technology provides for physical and psychological needs and wants: neither do they offer a broad experience of a diverse range of problem-solving strategies. Whilst they appeal to the interests and aspirations of a certain percentage of pupils, they also serve to alienate many children, particularly girls. Such courses clearly form a part of technological education, but in themselves could not provide the richness that a cross-curricular approach can offer.

The Assessment of Performance Unit in Design and Technology had this to say:

Design and Technological Activity
Assessment of Performance Unit
DES, 1987

The basic premise of design and technological activity is that, using materials, tools and systems, human beings can intervene to modify and improve their environment. Underlying this intervention is the motive of responding to human needs.

In an educational context, pupils pursuing this activity must learn to exercise a range of strategies, which are dependent upon the application of relevant knowledge and a variety of skills. The whole activity is governed and given meaning by the human values that surround the task.

From this premise, it follows that design and technological activity is not the preserve of any single curriculum subject, but rather refers to an activity that may be exercised in a range of subjects, albeit with different emphases.

Cross-curricular design and technological education, therefore, needs to take a broad range of starting points from the world of everyday products, places and communications – the materials, machines, devices, environments and systems which children use or have contact with in their daily lives and which help extend and enhance their own survival capabilities.

Choose an aspect of your present teaching programme and describe the particular elements of it which you consider might already be contributing to technological education in its broadest sense.

Education by design

In the previous session it became apparent that our current images of the world of design suggest that they are all very helpful in promoting the enterprise culture and the gross national product. But education is not just about producing a consumer-orientated ready-made workforce, so what contributions can design make to secondary schools? In considering this it is helpful to distinguish between an **awareness** of design and the **skills** of designing.

Design awareness
Design awareness is concerned with the word 'design' – used as a noun to refer to the everyday products, places and communications which surround us – things which have already been designed. It has become increasingly important to be able to discriminate effectively between the qualitative values of the artefacts, systems and environments which are made available to us. At the same time we need to be aware of the difference between what we believe we want and what we really need. Skills of subjective and objective critical analysis and awareness are now more than ever essential for successful survival.

There is also an enormous wealth of design history in the everyday things around us, providing opportunities for helping children to understand the evolutionary patterns of the social, cultural, political, economic and technical roots of the world they live in. Studying the shape and influence of the past helps develop an understanding of how and why things have come to be the way they are at present, and the ability to predict consequences of future change.

Design skills

How Designers Think
Lawson, B
Architectural Press, 1980

Design Methods: Seeds of Human Futures
Jones, J C
Wiley, 1980

When we begin to look more closely at the way in which designers think and act – 'design' as a verb, as a process – it becomes apparent that to a certain extent designers behave like scientists; analytical, investigative, rational, logical, objective, convergent and primarily concerned with the way in which the world is. At the same time, though, they also have to operate like artists; intuitive, spontaneous, expressive, subjective, divergent, and primarily concerned with the way in which people think and feel and how things might be. And they also operate in the professional world, taking risks, planning, organising, speculating and communicating effectively, and delivering the goods on time.

The skills of designing can be usefully, if artificially, categorised under a number of headings. There are a number of widespread variations of categorisation, but all the ingredients are essentially the same: evaluation, planning and organisation, investigation and analysis, imagining and developing ideas, and realisation and presentation. With perhaps one exception all of these skills can be already identified as happening in different subjects right across the curriculum, from English and art to physics and mathematics, though at present rarely in a connected and co-ordinated way.

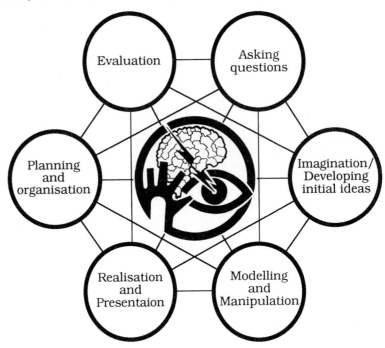

Within these design skills, however, it is the process of modelling which is not really effectively dealt with in any existing subject. Models are a great deal more than plastic construction kits: they are anything which can be described as 'simplified versions of reality'. Because they are simpler they are quicker and cheaper to create than the real thing, and they can therefore be more easily tried out, experimented with and manipulated. Words, numbers and drawing systems are models as well as three-dimensional structures: the skill lies in knowing what sort of model to use, and how much detail to include.

The most sophisticated modelling tool we have is actually our own brain. In what we call our 'mind's eye' we can create and change complex design ideas that combine 2D and 3D images, words and numbers, do so at speeds and levels of sophistication as yet unmatched by any single computer program, and then begin to speculate on the consequences of changing those ideas. In our 'imaginations' we can see shapes and forms in different colours, hear all sorts of sounds and experience a whole range of smells, tastes and textures; and even better, we can make the images move and change size, and control the volume and pitch of the sounds. There are, however, limitations to cognitive modelling. The amount we can see and deal with 'on screen' at any one time is, for most of us, limited and so the consequences of a change to one aspect of the design will not necessarily be followed through to the whole. It is also important to share ideas with others. For these reasons external, physical 'real-world' models are needed as well, which is why we need to write things down, represent measurements by numbers, and produce drawings and constructions of images and objects we have visualised.

So, the activity of modelling involves a constant interaction between modelling and manipulating ideas 'in the mind's eye', and then manipulating materials to model those ideas in the real world. Through the use of a series of different 'snapshots of reality' (notes, sketches, prototypes, etc), initial hazy visions gradually become sharply focussed design proposals. The activity of modelling lies at the heart of designing, and it is possible to develop pupils' abilities in the same way that the sciences emphasise the development of numeracy and the humanities emphasise literacy. The processes of modelling, and the other design skills are described in more detail in Session 4.

Through the use of a series of different 'snapshots of reality' initial hazy visions gradually become sharply focussed design proposals.

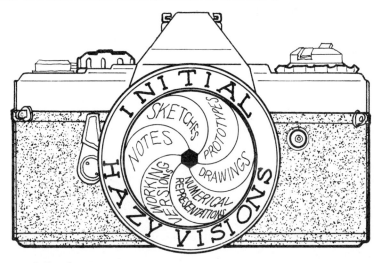

Processes of design

In too many schools over the past twenty years the design process has come to be crudely understood and presented as a systematic, largely unrelated linear sequence of problem-solving activities. Although it is true to say that designers do work through some sort of structure from a general starting point of recognising and understanding a problem towards a suggestion for a possible solution, they certainly don't progress in a rigid, routine and neatly-ordered manner. The process is much more complex even than the cyclic diagrams you might have come across. In practice there is a constant interplay between each of the skills, with a rapid changing of emphasis and a frequent switching between developing broad concepts and detailing and refinement. And, most important of all, the thinking strategies and tactics are always different for each problem and each individual designer.

In classroom terms, teachers need to try and achieve this subtle balance by indicating a strategy but permitting pupils to initiate their own tactical decisions, and to ensure that a diversity of themes and contexts provides a breadth of strategies.

A Design Process Model

No graphic model of the processes of designing could ever do full justice to the complex and unique way in which each individual designer works.

The traditional board game of Snakes and Ladders, however, provides an interesting analogy, illustrating perhaps something of the processes involved. The snakes represent unforeseen difficulties which are often encountered, and the ladders stand for the creative leaps which tend to happen when least expected. Chance and luck play an important part, and each game (or project) will follow a different pattern of progression while moving from start to finish.

Meanwhile the strands of the various design skills can be clearly identified permeating the project at every level. (The various methodologies referred to are described in more detail in Session Four).

Of course the game completely fails to model the essential element of skillful strategic and tactical decisions which the designer is able to make.

To play: start by identifying six human needs and possible opportunities to initiate change...

INVESTIGATION

DEVELOPING

FINISH
CONGRATULATIONS! YOU HAVE DEVELOPED YOUR CAPABILITIES. NOW START AGAIN WITH A NEW TASK 64

THINK OUT ARE FOR FURTHER DEVELOPMEN IF MORE TIME BECAME AVAILA

MAGAZINE ARTICLE DESCRIBES NEW MANUFACTURING PROCESS WHICH MIGHT BE OF USE 49

DIVERGENCE OF IDEAS

ILLUMINATIO
EUREKA

48

UNDERTAKE QUESTIONNAIRE TO DISCOVER PUBLIC RESPONSE TO PROPOSALS 33

TRANSFORM EXISTING IDEA INTO NEW POSSIBILITIES

QUICK THINKING - THROW AGAIN 32

CONSIDER ANALOGIES WITH THE PROBLEM

VISIT LIBRARY ESSENTIAL BOOK OUT ON LOAN

COMP A VISU AND VERI THEME SHE

INTERVIEW WITH AN EXPERT IS MOST HELPFUL 16

START
THINK OUT STARTING QUESTIONS AND SOURCES OF INFORMATION 1

DIVERGENCE OF IDEAS

AT1

AT2

DETAILED LEVEL (FOCUSSED PROPOSALS)

GENERAL LEVEL (HAZY SPECULATIONS)

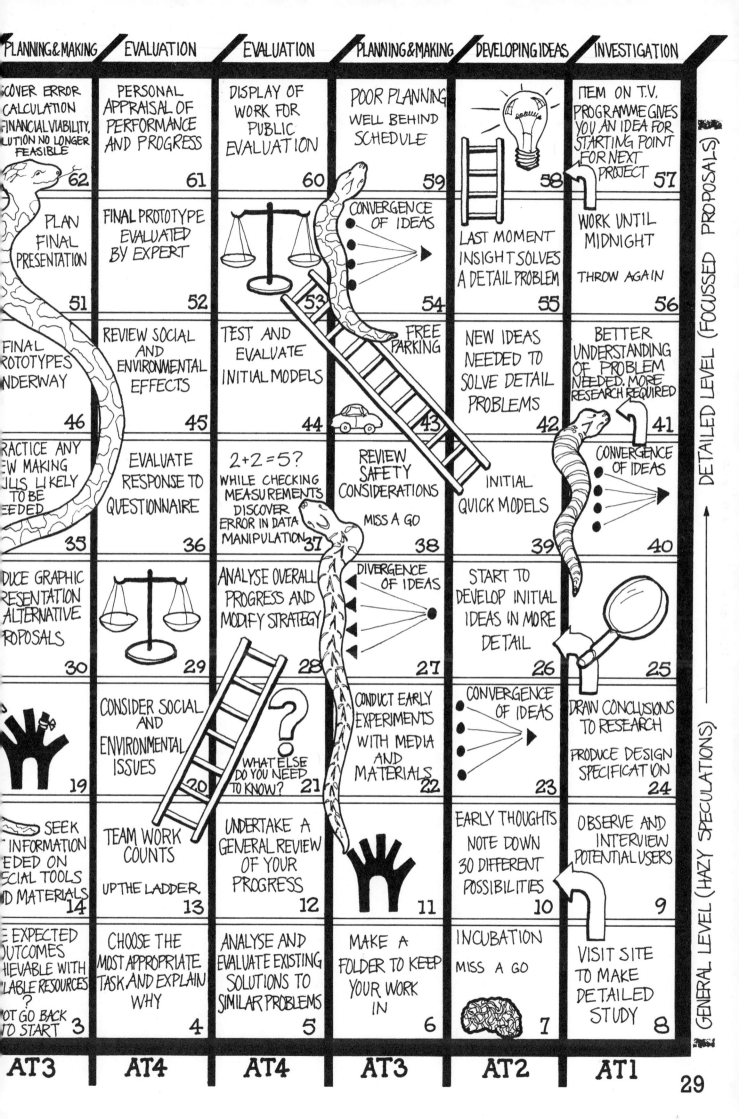

62 DISCOVER ERROR CALCULATION FINANCIAL VIABILITY, SOLUTION NO LONGER FEASIBLE

61 PERSONAL APPRAISAL OF PERFORMANCE AND PROGRESS

60 DISPLAY OF WORK FOR PUBLIC EVALUATION

59 POOR PLANNING WELL BEHIND SCHEDULE

58

57 ITEM ON T.V. PROGRAMME GIVES YOU AN IDEA FOR STARTING POINT FOR NEXT PROJECT

51 PLAN FINAL PRESENTATION

52 FINAL PROTOTYPE EVALUATED BY EXPERT

53

54 CONVERGENCE OF IDEAS

55 LAST MOMENT INSIGHT SOLVES A DETAIL PROBLEM

56 WORK UNTIL MIDNIGHT — THROW AGAIN

46 FINAL PROTOTYPES UNDERWAY

45 REVIEW SOCIAL AND ENVIRONMENTAL EFFECTS

44 TEST AND EVALUATE INITIAL MODELS

43 FREE PARKING

42 NEW IDEAS NEEDED TO SOLVE DETAIL PROBLEMS

41 BETTER UNDERSTANDING OF PROBLEM NEEDED. MORE RESEARCH REQUIRED

35 PRACTICE ANY NEW MAKING SKILLS LIKELY TO BE NEEDED

36 EVALUATE RESPONSE TO QUESTIONNAIRE

37 $2 + 2 = 5$? WHILE CHECKING MEASUREMENTS DISCOVER ERROR IN DATA MANIPULATION

38 REVIEW SAFETY CONSIDERATIONS — MISS A GO

39 INITIAL QUICK MODELS

40 CONVERGENCE OF IDEAS

30 PRODUCE GRAPHIC REPRESENTATION ALTERNATIVE PROPOSALS

29

28 ANALYSE OVERALL PROGRESS AND MODIFY STRATEGY

27 DIVERGENCE OF IDEAS

26 START TO DEVELOP INITIAL IDEAS IN MORE DETAIL

25

19

20 CONSIDER SOCIAL AND ENVIRONMENTAL ISSUES

21 WHAT ELSE DO YOU NEED TO KNOW?

22 CONDUCT EARLY EXPERIMENTS WITH MEDIA AND MATERIALS

23 CONVERGENCE OF IDEAS

24 DRAW CONCLUSIONS TO RESEARCH — PRODUCE DESIGN SPECIFICATION

14 SEEK INFORMATION NEEDED ON SPECIAL TOOLS AND MATERIALS

13 TEAM WORK COUNTS — UP THE LADDER

12 UNDERTAKE A GENERAL REVIEW OF YOUR PROGRESS

11

10 EARLY THOUGHTS NOTE DOWN 30 DIFFERENT POSSIBILITIES

9 OBSERVE AND INTERVIEW POTENTIAL USERS

3 ARE EXPECTED OUTCOMES ACHIEVABLE WITH AVAILABLE RESOURCES? NOT GO BACK TO START

4 CHOOSE THE MOST APPROPRIATE TASK AND EXPLAIN WHY

5 ANALYSE AND EVALUATE EXISTING SOLUTIONS TO SIMILAR PROBLEMS

6 MAKE A FOLDER TO KEEP YOUR WORK IN

7 INCUBATION — MISS A GO

8 VISIT SITE TO MAKE DETAILED STUDY

AT3 | AT4 | AT4 | AT3 | AT2 | AT1

DETAILED LEVEL (FOCUSSED PROPOSALS)

GENERAL LEVEL (HAZY SPECULATIONS)

The end-product

So, by asking pupils to use the work of the professional designer as a role-model, they will have the opportunity to develop more effectively a whole range of connected and flexible problem-solving related skills, particularly in terms of imaginative and real-world modelling and visual communication. A wide range of contrasting and complementary design-related activities, from engineering and architecture to the expressive arts and to marketing, is needed to ensure an experience of varying mixtures and amounts of each design skill. It is essential, however, to remember that design activity needs to have real meaning and value to the individual child, and that the role of the designer is only a model. The circumstances, pressures and needs of education are not the same as for professional practice and industry: in our world the most important end-products are the pupils themselves, not what they design.

Analyse the extent to which the content of your programmes of study are shaped by vocational or professional models, directly intended to prepare pupils for the world of work. Are these appropriately balanced by intellectual aims which emphasise the general experience and development of skills of thinking and doing?

Creativity in education

The word 'creativity' occurs frequently in the aims and objectives of many examination syllabuses and curriculum development projects. On closer inspection, the extent of the creativity which is actually delivered and assessed is often minimal. Few people in education really seem to understand what it involves, let alone how it might be encouraged.

As we discovered from the previous session 'The World of Creativity', a great deal more is now known about what actually makes people more creative in their thoughts and actions. Psychologists suggest that the abilities to think and act more creatively lie within us all, but have become blocked. Within our schools, the expectations of the traditional system of knowledge-based learning and the general attitude of valuing conformity above individualism, tends to inhibit the natural creativity which we observe and admire in young, pre-school children. Creativity is about taking risks, being able to accept failure, letting go, patience and persistence, flexibility, and removing boundaries. All that requires a confidence matured, reinforced and valued over an extended series of experiences − a double period a week in the art room is just not going to be enough. In the development of children's capacity to be more creative, we have a very long way to go.

Starting blocks

Obviously it is helpful to have a basic awareness and understanding of the nature of creativity, of the creative personality and of the creative process. Design and technological education provides many opportunities to enable children to explore and try things out to see what happens. One important role of the teacher is to permit, oversee and ultimately put the limits on such experimentation.

The attributes of creativity, or the lack of them, can also of course be recognised in children. For example, pupils whose creative abilities have not been blocked tend to take more initiative in the planning of project work, and in taking decisions for themselves. They are particularly resourceful when unforeseen situations occur. Frequently, it has been found, they prefer to work on their own, and are more strongly motivated by their own evaluation of the successes and failures of their work. Such children also are more likely to stand their ground in the face of criticism. When presented with complex difficult tasks they are generally optimistic, and tend to have the most ideas when a chance to express individual opinion is presented.

Pupils are conditioned to achieving success and excellence all the time – nothing but the best will do. Only when they are able to acknowledge that not every idea they have is brilliant will they start to experiment, take risks, and become less afraid of publicly admitting failure. A further important step is for children to be more freely able to make new connections between things which initially seem disparate. This is often difficult because we have become so used to labelling our world with definitions, classification systems and subject boundaries.

Our education system places a high emphasis on the excellence of ideas which famous and important people have had, and traditional discipline reinforces the idea that those in authority always know best. Older children in particular need to be encouraged to value their own ideas more than they do, and to believe in their own capability to design things which are in some way unique. A selection of techniques for stimulating creative responses is provided in Session 4.

Discuss the extent to which you consider your teaching style develops or inhibits the creative potential of pupils. Try and provide some specific examples.

and an increased yearly budget is of course likely to be advantageous, the lack of resources should not be used as an excuse for avoiding change in teaching content and style.

Design and technology blocks

It is going to be more difficult to deliver the requirements of the National Curriculum effectively in schools where rooms and workshops retain their discipline-specific identity (e.g. the woodwork room, technical drawing office) and are sited in different locations around the school. Unfortunately pupils tend to think and behave in the particular ways which relate to their expectations of the sort of work which normally goes on in a certain area and of the member of staff who usually teaches there. Starting to 'de-sign' classrooms by giving them non-subject specific names is an important step, though it takes a long time for established associations to be forgotten. Where new or re-designed accommodation is being planned then each main area should ideally contain a mixture of multi-media resources and facilities which enable both thought and action to take place. In other circumstances it might be worth utilising an ordinary space or classroom not normally used for a design and technology-related outcome, particularly for the introduction of the context and for the time when pupils identify and choose their task and outcome.

In planning places and spaces for design and technological activity extensive provision for storage of on-going and completed project work must also be given a high priority. It is easy to underestimate the amount of work generated, particularly when it accumulates over several years.

Safety regulations pose further problems, and it is important to ensure that pupils follow the correct procedures when using different workshop areas. Adequate supervision, which is more difficult with smaller groups of pupils doing different things in different places, must also be maintained.

How effective will the current facilities for integrated design and technological work be in your school? How can they be improved in the short-term without major expense? In the long-term what facilities will there ideally need to be?

Equal opportunities: gender

Providing equal opportunities in design and technology will involve a great deal more than providing facilities and access for girls to undertake wood and metalwork and for boys to learn about cooking and needlework. When given a free choice pupils still tend to adopt stereotype attitudes and so they also need to be actively encouraged and guided towards a broader range of tasks and potential outcomes. Where more structured teacher-led starting points are used it is essential that they are not perceived as gender-related: timetabling a group into the home economics area to work under the heading of 'the domestic environment', followed by a project in the CDT area making a 3D product within an 'industry' context must clearly be avoided.

How effective are equal opportunity strategies relating to design and technology in your school? How could they be most easily improved?

The art of design and technology

The contribution of art and design in any scheme being planned will be critical to the successful preparation of pupils for the aesthetics, imaging, generating modelling, and communication aspects of the programmes of study. It should also be remembered that many teachers of art and design have well established experience in planning, organising and assessing pupil-centred project work.

There are, however, two particular problems in the integration of art into programmes of work. First, although many art teachers will welcome the opportunity to contribute to design and technology, a proportion are likely to be resolutely opposed to the systematic and non self-expressive aspects. And secondly, many art teachers will quite rightly argue that, unlike CDT and home economics, they will eventually have their own separate National Curriculum requirements and commitments to meet, and that for them to teach design and technology as well will require extra staff, facilities and timetabling. Finding a way of successfully integrating art and design with other areas is, therefore, likely to pose particular problems for co-ordinators. Many teachers of art and design will need to be encouraged to review their role and priorities within the curriculum as a whole. At the same time attitudes towards art in other subject areas will need to change too: telling pupils to 'go and ask the art teacher what colour it should be' is unlikely to facilitate the sense of equality of partnership and co-operation which is needed.

In both philosophic and practical terms, how can art and design be most effectively integrated into design and technology in your school? Are there likely to be similar problems with information technology and business education?

Aesthetics and function

There is a common misconception that 'aesthetics' are concerned exclusively with appearance. Although the visual qualities of the made world do make the major impact on our emotional responses to our surroundings, aesthetics must also be said to apply to all sensory experience – of sound, touch, smell and taste as well. Designers, therefore, are not just concerned with shape, form and colour, but with all aspects of the products, systems and environments they create – the feel of a textured piece of paper, the 'resistance' of a volume control on a hi-fi unit, the magnetic 'pull' of a fridge door, for example. The fundamental role of the professional designer is to present technology in a way which is physically and psychologically acceptable to a human being (within the constraints of economic viability). Good designers don't so much design products as the experience of using them. This broader approach to the role of aesthetics, in which emotional response is an integral aspect of the purpose and success of the artefact, system or environment, is perhaps more widely understood in the field of ergonomics and marketing. Translated into classroom terms it suggests that 'aesthetics' are not the sole responsibility of the art teacher, and cannot be split from considerations of 'function'. It also reinforces the need for design and technological activity in school to be as much about people as machines and devices.

Re-read the sections in Session 1 which outlined the nature of technology and the role of the designer. Do your courses properly reflect a wholistic view of 'design and technology', or do they tend to separate the two?

Designing and making

Throughout the programmes of study pupils will need to develop a wide range of manipulative skills and processes in many different media, though these are not individually prescribed. Many of the examples given to support the programmes of study use the word 'make', which often tends to suggest the construction of three-dimensional items made in wood, metal, plastics, etc. which can be easily tested to see if they 'work'. 'Making' will however clearly need to be interpreted in a much broader way, particularly when dealing with the design of systems and environments. 'Realise', 'bring about', 'put into action' are perhaps more helpful phrases which permit and encourage the use of a wide range of appropriate materials and media.

How can non-full-size 3D outcomes be finally evaluated? Refer to the list of possible realisation media/project outcomes on page 12 (column 3) of *Introducing Design* and consider how each could be appropriately appraised.

The quantity/quality dilemma

The National Curriculum seeks work which is both broad and of quality. In discussing the role of 'craftsmanship' the insufficiency of time for 'perfection' as well as sufficient breadth to be achieved is recognised. Achieving the right balance between quantity and quality is always a difficult task, and will need frequent on-going analysis and discussion as courses evolve. At one extreme it must be argued that there is a danger of the traditional 'crafts' being lost within design and technology, and schools will need to ensure that this does not happen. At the same time it is useful to be aware of the limitations of our general use of the word 'craftsmanship' which we tend to apply to a standard of physical, manual work in a finished artefact, be it a chair, tapestry or model of a shopping precinct. When a pupil begins to demonstrate ability in working with such materials, increased standards of workmanship should be encouraged. For other children, with different interests and potential abilities, there are many other ways in which 'quality', or 'professionalism' can be achieved and observed across the breadth of design and technological work – through accurate observation, thorough investigation and understanding, efficient documentation, effective communication, and patient, persistent and determined application, perhaps. Of such qualities, that of 'appropriateness of action' is arguably at the heart of design and technological capability.

To what extent do your proposed courses achieve a good balance between the need for quantity and quality across a wide range of activity?

SESSION 4 Design skills

Introduction

Part of Session 2 discussed the way in which professional designers utilise a range of interrelated, process-based skills in order to identify and propose solutions to technological problems. Through the structured acquisition and development of these skills, pupils gain the ability to initiate change. Such design skills are not particularly special, and do not necessarily involve highly developed talents or 'gifts' – they are essentially simple extensions of everyday thinking and doing activities. *Introducing Design* presents the series of design skills which pupils will need to tackle the assignments in the book (see pages 7 to 16), and of course the requirements of the National Curriculum. This session provides further information on some of the concepts and techniques involved in each skill.

The text also indicates the average levels of progression in the development of design skills which might reasonably be expected across the 11 to 14 age range. A further level is also included, suggesting likely progression into fifth and sixth form work.

Refer to the National Curriculum programmes of study and identify approximately at which levels each of your current year groups are working.

Comparison with the National Curriculum programmes of study for each attainment target level indicates a high expectation of capability and content, clearly beyond those observed in the 'Stages of Development' sections presented in this session. A student currently undertaking an A level, or possibly even a degree course in a design-related subject, would be working to levels similar to those described in Key Stage 4, and would probably have a number of areas of weakness. However, it must be remembered that they are a statement of what should be expected of pupils who have followed a progressive course of study from the age of five to sixteen, delivered and co-ordinated by trained and experienced teachers. Also the 'average' child (defined in terms of technological capability, which is not necessarily the same as academic or intellectual capability) will only be expected to achieve levels 2, 3/4, 5 and 7 at the end of each Key Stage (1 to 4). It is, therefore, likely to be some years before such standards are achieved as presented (a child commencing Key Stage 1 in September 1990 will not be at GCSE level until June 2001), so interim strategies and expectations need to be adopted. Whilst the levels of capability indicated in this session are only generalised observations, rather than objectively researched and documented stages of progression, they may well be found to be a more realistic short-term guide and starting point for observation and discussion.

After an initial read-through during this session you will find it useful to refer back to these notes whilst planning, delivering and evaluating activities and programmes of study which utilise assignments from *Introducing Design*.

Different children in different circumstances will achieve very different levels of achievement and development. As you read through each of the skills, consider the extent to which the guideline stages of development reflect your own observations and expectations of what your pupils are or might be capable of achieving within each year group. Make notes of where you feel your experience of working with pupils in your subject and school seems to differ from the statements made in each section, and try and identify some specific examples to present and discuss with the rest of your group. You may well discover that pupils can effectively handle a particular skill in one subject area, yet find it difficult to understand and apply in another.

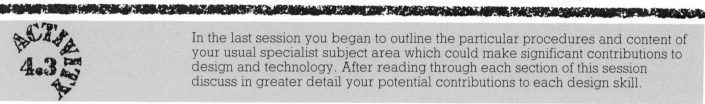

In the last session you began to outline the particular procedures and content of your usual specialist subject area which could make significant contributions to design and technology. After reading through each section of this session discuss in greater detail your potential contributions to each design skill.

Asking questions/investigation

Asking questions

Analysis of the context is needed before a programme of research can be drawn up. This involves the ability to ask appropriate questions about the situation – to identify what information needs to be found out. Unless the pupil has some general familiarity with the circumstances of the situation this will prove difficult, so it is important, particularly for younger children, that projects are based as far as possible within their everyday experiences. In *Introducing Design* a range of starting questions are provided. Wherever possible pupils should be encouraged to extend the list of questions at **any** point during the progress of their project.

Investigation

Investigation, or exploration, is concerned with finding out about, recording and analysing a situation in order to gain a better understanding and critical awareness of the human and technical circumstances involved. Historians, geographers and scientists and, from industry and commerce, ergonomists and market researchers are amongst those who have developed widely recognised investigative techniques which can be effectively used by children, provided they are suitably distilled. They can become involved in obtaining primary-source material, visiting and recording the environment concerned and consulting and observing the people carrying out whatever activities are involved; and retrieving secondary-source material in the form of visual, verbal and numerical information which has already been documented.

Design Methods Manual
Man-made Futures, Units 13-16
Cross and Rcy, 1975

The specific skills involved are not just of retrieval and documentation, but more:
- being able to ask the right questions of the right people in the right way
- ensuring that the levels of information sought and obtained are appropriate to the problem-situation being investigated
- choosing the most suitable methods of exploration and means of recording the information discovered.

When planning extended project work the following check list of research methods can be used. It is not essential for all of them to be covered in each project, but pupils should gain some experience of each at each level of the study programme. In an extended programme of research, however, pupils should be encouraged to obtain overall a mixture of **factual** information – size, shape, weight, cost, speed, etc; and other information which will be a matter of **opinion** – what people think and feel about things, their likes and dislikes, what they find important, pleasing, frustrating, etc. Some projects might involve hardly any research, particularly if pupils already know a lot about the problem-situation. In some cases this might be beneficial, as it will enable them to get rapidly into the stages of developing and realising their ideas.

User research
Could pupils observe and/or consult anyone who participates in, or is directly

involved with, the situation or a similar situation? To what extent might they be able to find out about:
- the things they do
- the way in which they do them
- how they think and feel about the circumstances they are in
- the opportunities they have to influence and change the circumstances of the situation.

What methods could pupils use to obtain and record this information? (sketches, diagrams, photographs, general interviews, questionnaires, experiments, etc.)

User trips

How can pupils' own impressions and experiences of the situation be documented? Are there any relevant activities they could try out for themselves to gain first-hand experience? Do they have any recollections of any previous similar experiences they have had?

Site study

In what ways could they document the environment in which the situation is? Which of the following will be relevant?
- historical and geographical factors
- sociological, economic, political information
- location
- layout, facilities
- sizes and spaces
- atmosphere – light, colour, texture
- the surrounding environment.

Existing solutions

Are there any other existing solutions to similar problem-situations which could be studied, analysed and evaluated? To what extent can these be organised on the basis of objective experiments?

Expert opinion

Are there any people who could provide 'expert' professional advice on any aspects of the situation? If the pupils don't know immediately of anyone, how might you or they set about finding somebody?

Literature search

Has any information about the situation, or a similar situation, been documented already in books, magazines, TV programmes, etc. If pupils are unlikely to have immediate access to such information where could they go to look for it? Don't forget to suggest the possibility of using information stored on a computer data-base.

Stages of development

Younger pupils generally lack the social skills necessary to conduct independent interviews with strangers, and indeed it would be most unwise to encourage them to do so. Thus user research activities are best restricted to identifying and discussing problems within class groups and with friends and other members of the family. Simple questionnaires can be effectively drawn up with a sample of about ten. Describing their own previous experiences can serve as the basis for user trips. With some projects it may be possible to invite outsiders in to school as stimulus and a source of information, or to take groups out of school under supervision. Instead of full-scale site studies, pupils should be directed towards a more manageable selection of elements to investigate. The evaluation of existing solutions (similar situations) can be introduced on a simple level, though children need considerable encouragement to evaluate critically as well as just describe.At a very general level a literature search can be undertaken, though this will usually need to be limited to visual and verbal information found within the resources of the school and the home.

The presentation of research work as **evidence** is important to emphasise at this stage. Theme sheets are effective for documenting general visual material. Work for projects with extended programmes of research should be documented in a reasonably formal co-ordinated report format.

Thirteen-year-olds become better able to sustain a more comprehensive programme of research, and should be able to build on previous experience to initiate some of the methods themselves. Activities such as writing letters requesting information, and making comparative studies of a wider range of neighbourhood locations, products and communications should be introduced. Information can be independently retrieved from local libraries. Towards the end of the fourth year pupils should be able to undertake an extended and broad programme of investigation, though some may still have problems choosing appropriate methods and limits, so careful guidance and monitoring is needed. A personal contact with a user or expert in the field can be most effective.

Fifth and sixth formers can be expected to generate and undertake comprehensive investigative activities. At this level an external contact often makes a significant difference to the overall success of the project.

Imagination/developing ideas of your own – 1

Imagination

Design Methods Manual
Man-made Futures, Units 13-16
Cross and Roy, 1975

Art Synectics
Roukes, N
Davis Publications (USA), 1984

GCSE Craft Design and Technology
pp. 10-11
Kimbell, R (Ed)
Thames/Hutchinson, 1987

We often ask pupils to 'use their imaginations' without really knowing exactly what we mean, or how to actually develop their ability to do so. Imagination is the mental ability to form images of external objects and events not actually present. Such images are predominantly visual, but can also include all our other senses, particularly auditory. Visual images are extremely important because they affect the rest of the body. It has been suggested that the stronger the image is, the greater the potential effect on the physical and behavioural response of the body. For example, athletes are known to have trained by visualising themselves winning before the start of a race, managers have imagined securing an important business deal before meeting the client, and patients have helped their recovery by seeing themselves well again. Everyone has the ability to form, hold, manipulate and record strong visual images, but most people have simply not practised and developed their ability since childhood.

Imagination is an essential ingredient of design, closely related to the ability to create new ideas and speculate on their potential success. It is also important in helping provide a strong self-image, confidence, a sense of direction, persistence and determination. Practising is not difficult – it is a matter of creating and concentrating on situations in one's mind's eye, picturing participation in the scene and paying close attention to the sights, sounds, tastes and smells. Mental role-playing (imagining being someone else) can be a good starting point.

Stages of development

Shipwrecked (p. 18)
Local issues (p. 33)
Human factors (p. 35)
Fantastic inventions (p. 41)
The domestic help (p. 55)

Many eleven- and twelve-year-olds are willing and able to imagine things with great vividness and to role-play convincingly and without inhibition when given the opportunity. By thirteen and fourteen the desire to use the imagination has begun to disappear in favour of logic and reason, but can still be powerfully externalised if sufficiently motivated and encouraged. Fifteen- and sixteen-year-olds who have not been exposed to regular practice have usually become very limited in their imaginative capabilities.

Developing ideas of your own – 1

This skill is concerned with the growth of the ability to identify a wide range of possible courses of action. It is here that creative thinking is primarily needed to establish new connections, and to transform existing ideas into new approaches. Thinking creatively is an attitude of mind. It involves:
- always being prepared to try new things out
- not worrying if things aren't always right first time
- not aiming to be a perfectionist
- making the most of whatever happens
- being patient
- long hours of struggle and self doubt.

All too often we put a blank sheet of paper in front of a child and say 'now be creative' and don't know what to do when their minds seem to go as blank as the piece of paper. There are, however, a number of recognised techniques, generally derived from management training procedures, for starting to re-stimulate the imagination and which can be effectively used with children. Like any skill they need to be practised frequently, regularly, consciously and deliberately to begin with, but it is often surprising how quickly children (and adults) start applying them intuitively. It is not recommended that they are done exclusively as independent exercises, or all at once: as far as possible they should form an integral part of longer-term projects. It should be remembered that there is nothing mystical or magical about these techniques. They simply reflect attitudes to natural processes of thought which most people have become unused to.

Brainstorming

Brainstorming is a good way of quickly generating a wide range of diverse ideas about a given subject, providing participants have some previous experience of the subject or problem. Although traditionally most successful when done verbally by a small group of people, the basis of its approach – that no idea should be evaluated or criticised at this stage – can be usefully applied by an individual. Simply always writing a long list of possibilities on a given subject can be helpful, and for this reason many activities and assignments in *Introducing Design* start with the compilation of an extended list. Sometimes a visual brainstorm, recording ideas as quick annotated sketches, can also be very effective.

Nothing new under the sun

Pupils often feel as though they are expected to invent something completely new, whereas designing is more to do with transforming existing ideas and bringing them together in new contexts. They frequently need to be reminded that 'there's nothing new under the sun', and to start looking for existing solutions to 'borrow' and adapt for their own purposes. At a later stage of development it can be worth systematically working through a series of **transformation words**, experimenting with changing the size, space, scale, form, function, style, direction, movement, etc.

Analogies

New and alternative approaches, insights and ideas can often be generated by the consideration of various analogies of the problem by posing the question 'what is it like?' This can be done most simply by substituting similar words for the common name or description of the object being considered, perhaps using a Thesaurus.

'Synectic' theory identifies four main types of analogy which can be applied:

- direct, in which the object is considered as being similar to the function of some other existing object: biological analogies are frequently interesting
- personal or empathetic, in which the designer imagines what it might feel like to be the object being considered
- symbolic analogies, relating to poetic, musical, visual or abstract metaphors
- fantasy, in which completely fantastic solutions are conjured up, sometimes revealing new insights to the nature of the situation being considered.

Happy accidents

There is a definition of design as being 'the opposite of chance'. But chance always seems to play an important part in the solving of a problem. Indeed some of the best things in life seem to happen to us by what we call chance. 'Serendipity' is described as 'the art of making happy and unexpected discoveries by accident'. Many twentieth-century artists, writers and musicians have successfully experimented with the use of chance in the creation of works of art, poetry and musical compositions. Such 'chance' occurrences are rarely completely consciously uninfluenced, but are subject to circumstances and limitations imposed by the creator, often without realising it.

So it can be worth actually trying to encourage pupils to create some 'happy accidents' by suggesting that they:

- go to a cupboard and take out the first thing they see
- open a dictionary at random and make a note of the first word at the top of the page
- turn on the television. What is the first image they see?
- re-arrange the letters of a keyword in a design problem to make new words.

Pupils should be encouraged to develop their own ways of generating random words. Whichever method is used they should then try to establish some connection, however remote or unlikely, with their problem and allow it to point them in new directions.

Letting go

There is an ancient Zen saying along the lines of 'If you want to attain something you've got to give up wanting it'. Providing we have thought about and struggled with a problem for a while it is often best to forget about it and allow our subconscious to start making the connections for us.

Stages of development

The concepts underlying these creativity techniques are far more abstract than those associated with any of the other design skills. For eleven- and twelve-year-olds it is the attitude, expectations and responses of the teacher which will be the most important in encouraging creative thought and action. With some prompting most pupils do not find it too difficult to 'brainstorm' quite extensive lists of existing solutions to problems they are familiar with. A few children can handle group sessions exploring potential solutions to problems, but many find this difficult at this stage unless the session is 'directed' by the teacher. Within the developmental stages of assignments it is important always to expect pupils to generate more than one possible solution to any intermediate problem posed, and these should be recorded on paper. Asking for six ideas usually manages to produce at least four alternatives without too much difficulty. Compiling a 'theme sheet' (as described in several assignments) is a good way of introducing the breadth of analogous, verbal and visual symbolic references to chosen topics, though at this level few pupils will produce sophisticated results.

It seems to be at around the age of 13 and 14 that children's creativity becomes most blocked. The demands for multiple solutions to be produced before decisions are made needs to be reviewed and reinforced, as pupils have started to narrow their vision. The teacher needs to prepare a convincing answer to the frequent response: 'my first idea is O.K. so why should I bother to think of any more?' The 'nothing new under the sun' approach also needs particular emphasis here as pupils often become convinced that they are expected to produce something totally original.

It is only with older pupils that a more direct presentation of creativity techniques can be effectively made, though still in the context of longer-term project work. Not all pupils will respond, but some do become readily able to generate ideas, make connections, and use visual and verbal analogies. Eventually it is possible to encourage the more experienced students to explore chance methods. The most able students do think and act in a more creative manner, achieving a successful balance with the more ordered processes of thought, but many retain a narrow vision.

Developing ideas of your own – 2: modelling and manipulation

Design: Processes and Products (T263 Unit 1)
Walker, D
The Open University, 1983

Design: Processes and Products (T263 Units 2-4)
Brown, S
The Open University, 1983

GCSE Craft Design and Technology pp. 14-15
Kimbell, R (Ed)
Thames/Hutchinson, 1987

Modelling and manipulation (getting down to details) deals with the capacity to externalise ideas and thoughts, and to construct and modify simplified representations of reality. In Session 2 we saw how the skill of modelling is at the heart of the design process. It is the basic procedure which enables a problem solver to move from the past, through the present and out towards the future.

A model is a simplified version of something else. Models are useful to designers because they are quicker and cheaper to construct and change than the real thing would be, and are therefore an effective way of predicting how reality might turn out to be. So, as well as the familiar idea of models being three-dimensional constructions of some sort, words, two-dimensional visual images (drawings, sketches, etc.) and numbers are all models too, because they are all capable of representing reality in a simplified way. Models can be used to change and manipulate:
- the **scale** of an idea by making the model smaller or larger than the real thing would be
- the **material**, by using something which is easier or cheaper to use
- the **form**, by exploring, for example, a three-dimensional idea in two dimensions, or by using words or numbers.

The designer of a car, for example, uses many different types of model during the process of developing ideas. Initial thoughts might well be externalised by words and numbers to describe the concept and specification of what is trying to be achieved overall. Later ideas may be expressed through sketches and drawings at many different levels of detailing and accuracy. Eventually full-size clay mock-ups will be produced, and a series of working prototypes. All these representations of the intended vehicle are models – simplified versions of reality. These physical models are in fact real-world representations of the models which exist in the car designer's mind. The process of developing the final design will have involved a complex interaction of thought and action, which will have progressed from initial hazy general speculations to detailed and tested refinements.

It is not just professional designers who use modelling techniques in this way. We all use conceptual and real-world models to solve everyday problems. Like most skills, the more we practise something the better able we are to do it. So the more experienced we become at using and choosing the most appropriate form of modelling to use, the more effective we become at solving problems.

Stages of development

All children engage in cognitive and real-world modelling activities without realising it, using drawings, words and numbers to describe and explore possible ideas. However they often need to be encouraged to actually manipulate them through further variation and development, and this needs to be consciously built into the structure of a project. There is also a tendency for pupils to leap from an initial sketch to a complex three-dimensional construction where simple intermediate paper or card prototypes would have been more beneficial. It is difficult at this level to observe and monitor cognitive modelling processes, although sometimes it can be seen implicitly in a sequence of sketches, notes or 3D models, or be discerned through conversation with the individual. Pupils continually need to be encouraged to externalise and document the processes of evaluation, modification and re-appraisal of their models, particularly 'mental' ones, which often turn out to be highly sophisticated.

Thirteen- and fourteen-year-olds do not seem to find the various modelling processes difficult in themselves, but lack the experience to judge which ones to use and when. They need to learn to analyse for themselves exactly what it is they are trying to discover by making the model so that they can then determine the most appropriate scale, material and form.

The concepts of modelling can be introduced and discussed explicitly with older pupils, though the use of prototypes of one sort or another remains frequently neglected even at this level: constant guidance is still needed if pupils are to construct, test, manipulate and modify real-world models effectively. With further encouragement pupils become better able to record cognitive experiences and, through reflection, analyse where ideas came from.

Modelling is one of the least well-recognised, -understood and -applied design skills in schools, and as such represents one of the most important areas for future development in design and technological education.

Realisation/presentation

Designer's Notebook
Bockus, B
Macmillan, 1977

Manual of Graphic Techniques 1
Porter and Greenstreet
Astragal, 1979

Manual of Graphic Techniques 2, 3 and 4
Porter and Goodman
Astragal, 1982, 1983, 1985

Introducing Design and Communication
Tufnell, R
Hutchinson, 1986

GCSE Design and Communication
Tufnell, R
Hutchinson, 1989

GCSE Craft Design and Technology
Kimbell, R (Ed)
Thames/Hutchinson, 1987

Presentation Techniques
Powell, D
Macdonald Orbis, 1985

Realisation is the process of turning ideas into some form of proposed reality. It demands that the designer comes to some form of conclusion (even though there may still be unresolved compromises and consequences) at a particular point in time, and that such conclusions are communicated to others. In a professional context a designer might need to produce 'realisations' at several stages to gain the further support of a client, or in educational terms, of the teacher.

Modelling, realisation and presentation are closely linked. There are subtle distinctions between the realisation of an idea produced by the designer through the use of real-world models, and the words, drawings and 3D models which are then used to communicate final proposals to other people. It is possible to identify three main levels of modelling, realisation and presentation:
- **personal**, in which the problem solver uses real-world models to conduct a dialogue with him or herself, or possibly other members of a design team during the development of ideas.
- **public**, in which the designer presents the general 'concept' behind a proposal in order to convince clients or potential clients of the potential of the solution to solve the problem, or to seek public opinion or support.
- **technical**, in which the designer must provide a set of clear, unambiguous instructions for those who will actually be constructing or implementing the proposals, and those who will be using or maintaining them.

Design Graphics
Fair and Kenny
Hodder and Stoughton, 1987

Desktop Publishing
Miles, J
Collins Desktop Publishing, 1987

Design and Communication
HMI publication
HMSO, 1987

How to Draw Machines
Butterfield and Ganeri
Usborne Books, 1987

On Camera
Watts, H
BBC Publications, 1984

The Usborne Cassette-Recorder Book
Bingham, K
Usborne, 1983

Your Cartoon Time
Harris, R
Knight Books, 1986

Manwatching
Morris, D
Jonathan Cape Ltd, 1977

In producing a realisation or presentation at a public or technical level all forms of communication media – verbal, visual and numerical – can be utilised. They are common to all three levels, though the formality and precision with which they are used varies at each level, as does the mixture of different techniques. In classroom terms, therefore, it is not simply a matter of dealing with the various techniques of communication, but trying to encourage pupils to become able to select the forms and formality which are appropriate to the particular circumstances of the problem and the 'client' (the teacher and/or examiner) and the pupils themselves.

Realisation/presentation media

Most of the following realisation 'conventions' are simplified descriptions of those commonly used by architects, engineers and three-dimensional designers.

Scale or full-size constructions
In circumstances in which the final solution, or at least a part of it, is to be three-dimensional, then clearly a 3D representation is likely to be particularly effective at the level of public communication. Deciding the scale, and the extent to which it will be a 'working' model, depends a great deal on the required focus of attention. In some instances it will be appropriate to make more than one model, perhaps using different scales to demonstrate different aspects of the design. Sometimes 'cut-away' models can be very effective, or ones where sections can be removed to expose internal workings. It is usual to use standard scale ratios such as 1:2, 1:50, etc. In the 'real world' there are sometimes conventions governing which to use, but in an educational situation at this level it is not necessary to follow them. Of course where possible 1:1 (i.e. full-size) models will give the most effective representation, and in the case of very small items the use of a larger scale (e.g. 2:1) should be considered.

The conventions of architectural modelling are fairly straightforward, generally utilising thin white card. The process of representing items intended for manufacture by a one-off scale model, however, presents much more complex problems of simulation. It is frequently more effective if different materials are used from those which the real thing would be made from, and it is often in the detailing that a block of wood or polyurethane is transformed into a completely different material and scale. Placing a model in context by adding a 'background' and some form of figure can add reality and a sense of scale. In the craft, or workmanship, sense, the development of model-making skills can be just as demanding as skills in carpentry, metalwork, etc.

Two-dimensional graphic work
Producing a visualisation (commonly known as an 'artist's impression') is often a quicker way of presenting a design idea to the public, and is particularly appropriate when time or resources prevent the construction of a three-dimensional model. Meanwhile technical drawings or diagrams are frequently used to communicate the precise details of proposals. There are a variety of graphic drawing conventions and systems which can be loosely interpreted for public presentations, but ought to be formally applied to technical information. All these systems are also very useful in the private 'modelling' stage, when they can be used as a rough sketch.

Presentation sheets are usually most effective when a mixture of the following techniques is used. A central image might, for example, be supported by a number of more detailed views, drawn at different scales, from different viewpoints and/or using different drawing systems and media.

Maps and plans show the relative spatial locations of places, or components of objects, from an imaginary two-dimensional 'bird's eye' viewpoint.

All change (p. 67)

at the start of each section.

Read through a copy of your current GCSE examination syllabus. Consider the extent to which the projects and lessons have been directly based on statements in the syllabus, or on its structure.

Comparison of the formal statements of most current GCSE syllabuses with the actual courses of study which take place frequently reveals that the content is being delivered through a range of starting points and activities generated by the teacher and the pupils, rather than the syllabus. It needs to remembered that the stated requirements of the National Curriculum and TVEI are the equivalent of a syllabus, and not a prescription for delivery. It is up to teachers to develop imaginative and exciting ways of putting broad and balanced courses of study together which are appropriate to the needs and resources of the pupils and staff of the individual school. Suitably tailored, *Introducing Design* could therefore be described as one approach which could appropriately form the starting points and activities for the significant part of such a course.

Design and technological teaching styles

Particular approaches to the process of teaching and learning are central to the delivery of design and technology in the National Curriculum and TVEI. These approaches are often described as being 'process-based', 'pupil-centred', 'experiential' and specifically not 'didactic' or 'teacher-led', although very little explanation or guidance is given as to what these terms mean. As it has become apparent, design and technological education is full of words which have different meanings to different people in different circumstances.

Making sense of the terminology

Read the following suggested explanations of some of the important differences between the meanings of words and phrases commonly found in TVEI and National Curriculum documents. Discuss the explanations within your group and aim to arrive at a common understanding of each term, with reference where possible to specific examples based on existing practices in your school.

Traditional subject-centred approaches place emphasis on knowledge content, whereas **process-based** approaches are more concerned with equipping the child with skills of independent learning, though usually within a specific area of content. **Pupil-centred** learning occurs when a teacher helps to shape and form a task identified by the student, or provides stimulus which is particularly appropriate to the previous experiences of the individual child at that particular time, rather than that of the group as a whole. **Independent** learning programmes offer a high degree of responsibility given to individual children to set and undertake their own learning activities, under the close guidance and supervision of the teacher. They often involve reference to resource packages which include written material, workbooks, videos and assignments. **Didactic** approaches usually mean hearing from,reading about or watching someone else who has undertaken a particular activity. **Experiential learning** is learning through the actual undertaking of a practical activity.

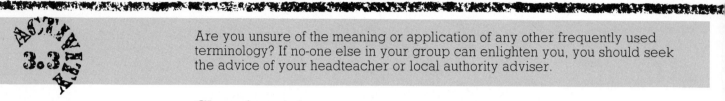

Are you unsure of the meaning or application of any other frequently used terminology? If no-one else in your group can enlighten you, you should seek the advice of your headteacher or local authority adviser.

New Ways to learn
Dacey, J S
Greylock (USA), 1976

Changing styles

Many teachers are unfamiliar with non-didactic teaching and learning styles; in addition to the many new general pressures, issues and problems to confront, and continued lack of resources to meet the new requirements, classroom teachers are also expected to re-appraise and change the things they do and the way they do them. Trying to adapt teaching style is probably the most difficult change of all to make, particularly as there is a direct correlation between a teacher's style and personality. The appropriateness of teaching style is, however, of fundamental importance to the success of design and technological education, and probably represents the most significant factor in the effectiveness of its delivery. Formal teacher-led approaches will not be adequate to enable pupils to work across a range of levels and programmes of study and to perceive the wholistic nature of the attainment targets.

You may already feel strongly that new teaching styles are to be welcomed or challenged. This section is intended to help you to increase your awareness of the extent to which you might have to adapt your existing style. Although a complete change of style may not be necessary, most teachers will find that, to a greater or lesser extent, they will need to adapt their approach to the way they operate in the classroom.

In philosophical terms, most teachers tend to see their classroom role in one or more of a number of ways. Each role requires a different perspective on the authority of the teacher, and usually relates to the degree of direct control and influence on the classroom situation which the individual feels he or she wants to have.

What type of teacher are you? Think of a recent project-based or problem-solving activity you have led and consider which of the following groups of statements best describes the way you teach:
- passing on useful knowledge for later life
- always checking instructions have been precisely carried out
- not expecting to have instructions questioned
- wary of giving too much praise in case pupils feel over-confident
- unwilling to trust pupils to work without supervision

- discussing and negotiating lesson/project planning with the class
- encouraging group work
- praising and criticising in as balanced a way as possible
- emphasising value-judgements and promoting caring and responsible attitudes towards living

- believing pupils should be given a high degree of freedom
- insisting pupils take their own decisions
- always expecting pupils to generate their own goals
- not operating any system of external appraisal of progress and performance.

Because design and technological learning is not knowledge-based an exclusively traditional academic approach would not be very effective, although there will be situations in which the teacher needs to impart knowledge, and pupils ought to feel able to switch to a passive, receptive and respectful attitude as and when appropriate. Whilst the use of the word 'taught' in the National Curriculum documents is stated not to mean 'to imply that the material should be covered in a formal didactic way', the emphasis on completely open-ended, child-centred project work might seem to suggest an entirely liberated approach with pupils 'doing their own thing' all the time. There are, however, also clear suggestions that, particularly at lower levels, some tasks will need to be prescribed and thus more teacher-led.

Generally pupils need clearly defined structures and frameworks to move freely around in, and goals to work towards. Occasionally such strategies need to be completely initiated and developed by the individual pupil, but at most other times a general sense of direction and purpose needs to be provided by the teacher. What is needed, therefore, is a flexible mixture of teaching styles – a complex and subtle balance of instruction, guiding, and standing back.

Below are a number of statements describing some of the qualities of the sort of teaching style most appropriate to design and technology. Tick those statements which you feel already apply to your current practice and identify a specific example drawn from your classroom experience which illustrates such an emphasis.

Do you feel yourself to be primarily concerned with:
- ☐ providing opportunities for pupils to assume some responsibility for their own learning
- ☐ helping students to find information out independently, and to make the best use of available resources
- ☐ encouraging children to learn by exploration and discovery, asking questions, testing possibilities
- ☐ providing opportunities to identify and suggest solutions to open-ended, real-life problems, with no expert's 'correct' solution
- ☐ presenting clearly defined objectives, but not related to specific areas of knowledge
- ☐ discussing and negotiating details of work-requirements with individual pupils
- ☐ taking into account the child's own assessment of work and progress
- ☐ facilitating and valuing co-operative team-work
- ☐ encouraging group discussions and peer group evaluation
- ☐ talking and communicating with children on equal terms
- ☐ supporting decisions taken by students, and respecting their considered judgements
- ☐ involving pupils in administrative decisions
- ☐ encouraging informality
- ☐ being willing to vary the intended structure of lessons to maximise on unplanned learning opportunities
- ☐ when it happens, being willing to admit ignorance on a particular subject
- ☐ being keen to work in team-teaching situations.

Go through each statement with the other members of your group and compare the examples you each thought of.

There have been two main purposes to these activities. The first is for you to become more aware of the way in which your teaching style compares or contrasts with your colleagues', and the second is to help you identify the extent to which you will need to aim to modify your style.

It may well be by this stage that you feel you have no real wish to make such changes, and would find them extremely difficult and intolerable. If you have not already done so, you should make your colleagues aware of your reservations so that further appropriate INSET courses can be provided for you, and your reservations can be taken into account in the planning of curriculum development initiatives: this will help to establish situations where the strengths of your style will be most valuable. New teaching styles cannot be developed overnight, and teachers who feel threatened either by having to let go of some of their authority, or by the need to have to exert more direction and structure, will need a lot of support, encouragement, patience and understanding from their colleagues.

It also needs to be recognised that teaching styles suitable for design and technological education are a great deal more demanding than the comparative order and control of 'traditional' styles of learning. They are only really feasible if group sizes do not exceed twenty. Extra time is essential to facilitate the preparation of resources and workspace, and, most importantly of all, frequent and effective communication between participating staff. In situations where it does work, however, standing back and watching groups of highly motivated children using their own initiative and resources to extend their experiences and capabilities significantly is an experience that few teachers forget in a hurry.

De-signing design and technological education

Within professional practice design consultancies are starting to remove some of the traditional boundaries which define the territories of designers. By changing, or **de-signing** the common labels of 'graphics', 'architecture', 'engineering', 'fashion', and so on, designers are increasingly not just concerned with creating individual products, places and communications in isolation, but as components of larger environments and systems.

This section examines the clear parallel which can be made to the development of cross-curricular work in secondary education. To reveal and gain access to the whole it is necessary to move away from perceptions of traditional subject labels and create new, much broader **contexts** and **outcomes**. Within each existing subject area teachers need to be more aware of their more general roles, whilst still representing and contributing their specialist knowledge when called for.

Design and technology right across the curriculum
To begin with it is again important to have a clear and agreed understanding of the meaning of the terminology being used. The words and phrases 'multi-disciplinary', 'inter-disciplinary', 'integrated' and 'cross-curricular' are often confused. **Multi-disciplinary** activities occur when teachers representing different subject areas base a programme of work on a common theme, though continue to work separately through and for their own subject syllabus. For example, in art pupils might produce visual studies based on 'life in the trenches', whilst in English they study and write poetry 'from the front line', and discuss the political and economic issues in history. In **inter-disciplinary** work, the links between the subject areas are stronger, and thematic work might involve common stages of investigation and possibly development. The end-products, however, are still rooted within the requirements of the discrete subject disciplines. Thus a group visit to a local village observing and recording historical, geographical and biological information and leading to the production of three separate projects would be an inter-disciplinary study. **Integrated work** (e.g. integrated science, integrated arts) differs significantly from multi- or inter-disciplinary activity in that the traditional subject bases are transformed into new groupings, and thus the focus of the activity does not necessarily contribute to the boundaries of the traditional subject syllabus, but to wider, though still defined, limits. Meanwhile **cross-curricular** work potentially spans the whole curriculum, and cannot be discerned as the property of any specific traditional subject or group of subjects. In both these approaches individual teachers may

still to a certain extent represent their own specialisms, but are nonetheless seen as making a contribution to the whole.

Identify any projects undertaken at your school which could each be described as 'multi-disciplinary', 'inter-disciplinary', 'integrated' or 'cross-curricular'.

Whilst TVEI initiatives have promoted work which is completely cross-curricular, the National Curriculum working party have placed less emphasis on such an approach. Although the terms of reference of the working party described design and technology as an activity which goes 'across the curriculum', their Consultative Report appeared to focus on activities which spanned and co-ordinated art and design, CDT, home economics, business studies and information technology, and which on occasion drew on the 'specialist knowledge and skills of other foundation subjects' and contributed to economic and career awareness, business understanding, environmental awareness, and health and safety education.

Thus the National Curriculum approach is perhaps more 'integrated' than 'cross-curricular' (though it clearly goes beyond 'multi- or inter-disciplinary'). Although such an emphasis may not have been intended, such statements do not, therefore, seem to endorse and actively promote the TVEI perception of design and technology as a dimension of the whole curriculum and as a focus for subject-suspended, cross-curricular project work. With effective co-ordination all subjects have a great deal to contribute and benefit from a broad approach to design and technology, and, whilst more ambitious, such a strategy should seriously be considered. Ideally a number of projects should be undertaken in which teachers of English, history, physics and so on work together with design and technology teachers in different mixtures of non-subject-specific ways. Meanwhile the requirements for programmes of study in history and geography and guidelines for art, music and PE will need to be closely cross-referenced to ensure that there is no bias towards science, mathematics and English.

Design dimensions of the curriculum

Whilst the text and assignments in *Introducing Design* cover integrated work in art and design, CDT, home economics, business education and potentially in information technology, they also explore relationships with other subjects. It is within truly cross-curricular, project-based work that pupils can most effectively explore the way in which the skills, knowledge and values generated in their other subjects (and in experiences both in and outside school) naturally connect together to form the real world in which they live. Indeed it is the ability to make links between seemingly disparate elements (traditional subject boundaries) which is the basis of the creative thinking that needs to be encouraged, and it is the 'survival' themes, and the contexts, environments and situations which provide the starting points for activities, which help reveal connections.

On a traditional subject-by-subject basis it is possible to identify at a very general level the existing and potential contribution of each to the development of process-based design and technological awareness and capability, representing the design dimension of the curriculum. The potential contributions summarised and listed here are not necessarily exclusive to that subject, but are those which are usually given particular attention and emphasis. Neither are they necessarily the only contributions of each subject.

The following activities are intended to help you explore the design dimensions which already exist within your present practice, and to learn more about the way in which other subject areas make a contribution. It will also help you map and begin to develop a more co-ordinated and progressive skill-based structure across the curriculum.

The lists below are summarised versions of the main potential contributions of each subject area to the development of skills in design and technological awareness and capability. They do not include knowledge-based content. Extend and elaborate on the potential of your specialist subject area(s). Analyse some examples of your existing programmes of work to illustrate and clarify the contribution you already make, and those which, by a simple extension of your present practice, you could start to provide. Present what you consider to be your existing subject area's potential contribution to the rest of your group. You might be surprised to find unexpected areas of overlap. Try and identify common contributions, and clarify the extent to which similar skills are being covered. Are similar or different standards expected through the various age ranges?

Summaries of the design dimensions of traditional subject areas

Art and design
- the investigation and analysis of primary source material, recorded through the use of visual images, leading to the development and realisation of ideas
- the imagination, manipulation and transformation of visual images, both in the 'mind's eye', and in the real world
- visual and tactile aesthetics in two and three dimensions
- the understanding of the expressive, emotional qualities of line, shape, form, colour and texture
- the concepts of visual analogy, transformation, symbolism and culture
- subjective evaluation
- pupil-centred, project-based learning

Craft, design and technology
- the analysis of problems of function and aesthetics with closely defined constraints
- the recognition of the need for functional and aesthetic solutions to co-exist
- the evaluation of objective performance qualities of existing and proposed solutions
- application of scientific principles which can be utilised in the solving of problems
- the awareness of the operational characteristics of materials and tools, and developing skills in their use
- the concepts of workmanship, and accuracy through refinement
- the need for precision in the communication of technical information
- the planning and organisation of project work over a given time-scale

Home economics
- the solving of problems in a domestic and community context, with particular reference to food choice and preparation, health and clothing, interior design, consumerism and marketing, child development and the needs of the handicapped and elderly
- the investigation and analysis of existing solutions to problems
- the transformation and development of ideas for proposed solutions to problems, with particular reference to cost-effectiveness, convenience, durability, safety, hygiene
- the modelling, testing and evaluation of ideas in a scientific manner
- the communication of proposed solutions at general and technical levels

Business education
- an awareness and understanding of market forces, financial services, enterprise initiatives, company organisation, supply and demand, product development, and advertising and marketing
- the need for team-work and detailed planning and organisation
- the effective use of available resources (including people)
- the benefits and disadvantages of mass-production to the designer, manufacturer and consumer, and the control of quality

Information technology
- the retrieval of information from databases
- the analysis of systems
- the practical application of graphic modelling, and in two and three dimensions
- the use of spread-sheets, word-processing and page-making facilities
- the presentation of information
- the generation and editing of sound and video images

Working in your group, and with specific reference to the design and technology 'knowledge' and 'value' areas of the programmes of study at each level, investigate and discuss the cross-references which need to be made between the National Curriculum requirements for each foundation subject.

ACTIVITY 3.9

Choose a number of assignments from *Introducing Design*. Analyse the extent to which various existing subject areas could most effectively contribute towards the implementation of each.

Mathematics
- the manipulation of numerical models
- the measurement of shapes and solids
- the use of networks, structures and patterns
- the practical application of measurement of changes of scale, volume and area
- the prediction of behaviour of objects
- problem-solving strategies within certain constraints

Sciences
- the development of an investigative and analytic approach
- the production of evidence to support a hypothesis
- the generation of experimental curiosity
- how the natural and man-made world works physically, chemically and biologically
- communication through recording of tests, results, explanations and conclusions

English and other language work
- development of skills of composition, imagination, verbal accuracy, clarity, brevity, sequencing and structure
- the development of critical analysis in the evaluation of experiences of everyday products, places and communications
- the consideration of editing and layout in presentation in situations where words and visual images closely interrelate
- the use of analogies, metaphors and word-play techniques in the generation and expression of ideas

Drama/Media studies
- the exploration of issues of human relationships in a man-made world through role-playing and expressive work
- the development of the imagination
- the bringing together of story-telling, music and acting with the design of stage movements, sets, costumes, and lighting
- working together as part of a team
- the critical analysis of existing communications
- the development of related visual and verbal narratives

Music/Dance
- an understanding of the emotional response to pattern, rhythm, tone, texture and structure
- the application of formal and informal processes of composition
- communication through conventional and experimental notation
- physical co-ordination and expressive response
- realisation and presentation through performance

PE/Sport
- awareness of physical and mental capabilities and limitations of the human body relating to performance and health
- task-related problem-solving
- team-work
- recreational contexts and needs

Geography/History
- primary- and secondary-source information retrieval and documentation
- the inter-relationship of elements in a system
- a comparative awareness of different past and present societies and cultures and evolutionary behaviour patterns, with particular reference to food, transport, shelter, community and resources, and to economic and political events
- an insight into how people have thought and felt about and reacted to changes in products, places, communications and systems

Foreign languages
- role-play problem-solving situations
- communication skills
- differing customs and cultures of other countries

Contexts and outcomes in design and technological education

Identifying contexts

All design and technological activity is prompted by needs and opportunities for change within a **context, situation or environment**. Pupils needs to be aware of and understand the context they are designing for, so that it is perceived as the starting point. Over a period of a year or so, projects should cover a broad range of situations which provide opportunities to deal with a variety of issues and contexts, such as:

- the home and community
- local industry and commerce
- the natural and made environment
- leisure and entertainment.

When planning a complete programme contexts of varying scales will need to be incorporated, from a single classroom or office at one extreme to perhaps a town centre at the other. Wherever possible pupils should have or gain first-hand experience of each environment or situation, but where this is not possible, secondary-source material should be substituted, such as video material and resource packs, along with imaginative role-play exercises and visits from outsiders.

A range of contexts are identified within the National Curriculum, though it is acknowledged that it will often be difficult to draw sharp distinctions between them – a home and a school are both parts of a community, for example, and recreational activities could be common to all contexts. So the design of, say, a pocket torch might be the outcome of the study of home or industry, whilst a puppet show about road safety for schoolchildren could have been derived from a school, community or recreational context. At the lower levels a higher percentage of contexts should be ones with which pupils already have some familiarity, though as they become older the contexts should be increasingly 'other people's', and a higher proportion should relate to commerce and industry. The assignments in *Introducing Design* provide an appropriately broad range of contexts, and the main section headings (Food, Shelter, Transport, etc) could be used as a structure to ensure the delivery of further breadth.

Identify the possible context(s) for each of the following assignments in *Introducing Design*:

- Listening in (page 47)
- Fun and games (page 60)
- All change (page 67)
- Saver return (page 81)
- Off the peg (page 90)
- Back to nature (page 100)
- Moonbase (page 110).

Identify a number of specific local contexts which you consider could form the basis of an open-ended project. Some general suggestions are:

- a hospital or clinic
- a park or play area
- a transport terminus
- a factory
- a row of shops.

As a group select one context and a lower school year group, and anticipate a range of assignments (tasks and outcomes) which might develop. You might find it helpful to use the survival headings (shelter, food, clothing, etc.) used in *Introducing Design*. Working through the programmes of study, speculate on how the different tasks relate to the various areas.

Choosing the context, task and outcome

While it should be ensured that a number of contexts are unfamiliar, pupils are, however, likely to respond considerably more effectively to a context which has some relevance to their own needs and experiences, interests, and/or to issues of local and current concern. Ultimately older pupils should become able to identify their own contexts, and the resulting potential range of problems and projects, with a high level of independence. To do so successfully is, however, one of the most sophisticated design skills of all, requiring considerable experience of the ability to match expected outcomes with the requirements of the levels of achievement expected. Because *Introducing Design* is aimed specifically at 11- to 14-year-olds it does not, therefore, generally invite pupils to identify their own contexts, but instead provides opportunities for them to develop the ability to recognise design and technological tasks and outcomes within given situations.

It is, however, important to provide pupils with a structured programme of increasing freedom and responsibility for content and procedure. In practice this needs to be achieved in a balanced way at each level. Eleven-year-olds should undertake a number of open-ended projects as well as activities which are much more directed and structured. Generally, lower-school introductory projects benefit from being well-structured, in that a common theme can be explored together, and the general direction of development is towards a similar end-product, system or environment. However, provided children know something of the situation they are dealing with, supported perhaps by some imaginative preparation, they are quite capable at an early stage of choosing from a list of prescribed tasks which ones to tackle, and indeed should be encouraged to do so. They should also be given the opportunity of suggesting directions of their own which can be negotiated with the teacher.

For 13- and 14-year-olds a common, directed context or theme and research programme normally remains the most effective, followed by fairly well-structured development to ensure that preparatory stages are not missed. A much wider scope of choice of end-product becomes possible, however. Alternatively a context can be stated, but the choice of thematic content left to pupils to identify. Practice in identifying 'starting questions' (see below) is always useful, and can be occasionally undertaken as an isolated exercise. Whilst the direction of many assignments may well become generated by the individual pupil, some short-term activities should still be teacher-led. When a choice of task is offered the teacher needs to guide the pupil towards the one which will produce the best possible results in terms of the pupil's personal interests and capabilities, and the resources (information, tools, materials and time) which are readily available.

The most able pupils are likely to have become able to identify contexts and potential outcomes for themselves during the course of their fourth year, though they will still need careful guidance. By the start of the fifth year most pupils can be invited to consider a number of possible projects, and be expected to generate a reasonable list of starting questions. Whereas the general nature of the end-product might be influenced by personal interest, it must be balanced by the sound basis of a broad programme of primary- and secondary-source research. Close guidance is still needed to ensure that there is adequate scope for investigation, and that appropriate limits are set. It is possible for the student to be too familiar with the problem-situation, and rely too much on his or her own perception, and propose solutions which do not take other people's needs into account. Sixth formers, as part of their course, should be expected to generate projects themselves, but weaker students will continue to find this difficult.

Choosing and starting projects

When pupils have the opportunity to select tasks for themselves, either completely, or from a given list of themes, topics or activities, they will need to make a careful choice. The ability to identify appropriately contexts and situations for design and technological activity is closely linked to the growth of the process of initial analysis (asking questions) and the recognition of potential sources of information (investigation).

Design Project Guide
Man-made Futures, Unit 12
Roy, R
Open University Press, 1975

Completing a **Project Proposal** form (p. 94) is a valuable exercise, providing a clear structure for the students, and a good indication for the teacher of their level of existing awareness of the problem and appropriate sources of information. Under **Statement of Problem**, the basic situation should be described as concisely as possible: starting with the phrase 'There is a problem in that. . .' can be a useful way of generating such a statement. The list of **Starting Questions** will initially identify and record all the areas which the student recognises will need investigation. **Sources of Information** should provide details of where it is expected that answers to the starting questions are likely to be found. These can be effectively categorised under the headings used on pp.57--8. Finally, **Expected Outcomes** should provide a statement as to the form in which the final design proposal might be realised (e.g. as a series of drawings, models, or a performance, etc.). Where a student, and teacher, discover that only a few starting questions have been generated, or that the sources of information are limited or vaguely defined, it suggests that the project is unlikely to be a suitable one to choose.

Project outcomes: artefacts, systems and environments

The National Curriculum requires pupils to undertake tasks which result in the design of a range of different types of outcome. There is likely to be some confusion as to the distinctions between artefacts, systems and environments. To a certain extent there is a hierarchical relationship between them. An **artefact** is usually considered to be a single two- or three-dimensional object 'produced by manufacture' (i.e. a 'product' or 'communication' as described in *Introducing Design*). A **system**, meanwhile, is an 'inter dependent organisation of parts' – that is to say, something which uniquely exists as the result of a particular relationship between a number of artefacts, people and/or events. A school timetable, a co-ordination of kitchen units and appliances, or the programme of events for a school fête could therefore all be described as being systems. Finally, an **environment** is the situation and surroundings in which a system, together with other systems and products, operate – in other words, indoor and outdoor places and spaces such as classrooms, bus stations, theme parks etc. Thus some outcomes might naturally involve a combination of design of products, systems and environments.

To analyse a further example:
● an engine, wheel and chassis are all artefacts
● a car (being an interdependent organisation of those artefacts) can be said to be a system
● a car park can be described as an environment (one of many surroundings in which cars operate).

However, it could also be said that:
● a car is an artefact
● a car park (being an organisation of cars, lorries, parking bays etc) is a system
● a town centre is an environment in which a car park operates.

and that:

- shafts, pistons and valves are all individual artefacts
- an engine is a system (an organisation of shafts, pistons and valves)
- a car is an environment in which an engine, and other systems and products operate.

The example can be extended further in either direction of scale. For general purposes, most project outcomes can be easily and commonly identified and agreed as being an artefact, system or environment, but this does represent a 'grey' area which may lead to a lack of breadth of content, particularly where an individual teacher is used to dealing with outcomes of a limited range of scale and number. *Introducing Design* contains a wide range of activities which cover artefacts, systems and environments, or various combinations of such outcomes.

With reference to *Introducing Design* establish the type(s) of probable outcome of the following assignments:
- Planning your own city (page 33)
- Soap opera (page 52)
- Joyful noises (page 59)
- Symbols and logos (page 78)
- Terminus (page 82)
- Roboritual (page 92)
- Futurehome 2000 (page 109)

For each of the following outcomes identify the possible original context(s) and whether the outcome(s) could be described as artefacts, systems or environments:
- a mobile computer workstation
- a mural for a classroom in the school
- display stands for a local company
- a Hallowe'en party
- a tape-slide show about the history of a local church
- the re-design of the backyard of a local shop
- a musical revue based on the 1960s
- an item of personal adornment.

Planning and structuring the curriculum to facilitate design and technological education

It will be some years before the majority of secondary schools are fully able to implement tried and tested, co-ordinated and progressive programmes of cross-curricular design and technological education. Until then a certain amount of experimentation is needed, building on and enhancing existing practice, and undertaking change on a small scale, arising from the particular strengths of existing good practice within each school. It would not, therefore, be appropriate at this stage to try to devise an overall plan which defines a permanent structure. It does, however, need to be ensured that the different initiatives which are undertaken do begin to explore a wide enough range of content, methodology and activity.

Co-ordinating the whole experience
Without doubt effective management of courses will be essential to success. In

most schools a central co-ordinator will be needed, probably supported by a group of key teachers. The co-ordinator will need to be an experienced teacher with a background in a wide range of design and technologically-related disciplines, and to be seen as part of the senior management team of the school. The scale of the task should not be underestimated as it will involve directing school-based INSET, uniting and leading a team of teachers, co-ordinating programmes of study and assessment procedures, and overseeing the allocation of resources. Close liaison with the timetabler will be of utmost importance to ensure the appropriate blocking of staff, pupils, time and rooms.

As an overall strategy, co-ordinators and planning groups should ensure that during each key stage of the National Curriculum pupils receive a balanced programme of:
- short-, medium- and long-term assignments
- small-, medium- and large-scale contexts
- activities which involve the use of a differing range of design skills and strategies, resulting in a mixture of artefact, system and environmentally-based outcomes
- technology-based themes and topics
- opportunities for individual and group work
- use of a wide range of appropriate tools and realisation media.

Such a programme is likely to be delivered in a variety of ways, such as:
- short intensive programmes occupying a number of full days (up to a week) during which part, or all, of the normal timetable is suspended, and many subject areas contribute
- following a general introductory session, several subject areas combine, or each deals with different topics in non-subject specific ways, occupying between a half or whole term
- spread across a regular, specific two-, three- or four-period 'cross-curricular' slot on the timetable, lasting between a half or whole term
- being dealt with as an extension of part of the existing provision of a specialised subject.

Using the assignments in *Introducing Design*, together with any others you are familiar with from your existing practice, try and draw up an initial possible and desirable programme of activities for first year pupils which meets at least most of the criteria above. Then progress to year two and make sure any elements omitted in year one are delivered, and so on. Do not let the structure of the existing timetable influence your decisions at this stage, as it is your recommendations which will need to be accommodated in the drawing up of future timetables.

You might find it useful to begin by reading the following imaginary case study of a planning group considering their Key Stage 3 programme for the first time. Because the circumstances of each school will be entirely different, it should not in any way be thought of as an ideal model. Neither does it really discuss the considerable organisational implications of such a programme. It serves simply to indicate the way in which a variety of contexts and methods of delivery need to be utilised, and the potential complexity of running and co-ordinating such a programme.

Case study
It was suggested that in the first year one afternoon a week be devoted to completely cross-curricular programmes of work. Initially all classes would undertake the 'Shipwrecked' assignments. At various times pupils would experience open-ended and more directed approaches, sometimes working with individual members of staff, sometimes with small teams of teachers. Each

activity would use a thematic 'survival' heading, and not a subject title. The project would be concluded at the end of the term with an exhibition of work. During the first three weeks of the spring term, pupils would undertake the introductory activities from the general theme of 'Food' and then for the remainder of the term tackle 'Back to Nature'. In the summer term work would be devoted to the study of a local village, culminating in the speculation of the effect of a planned new by-pass (this was an established first year project, extended along the lines of assignments in the 'Community' section of *Introducing Design*). At the very end of term, the timetable would be suspended for three days, and given over to a cross-curricular theme of 'Schoolscapes' (cf. worked example on p. 78).

Pupils would also have a further double period a week of design and technology led by teachers of art and design, CDT, home economics and information technology. Because of a lack of business education staff for the lower school it was decided that these aspects would have to be dealt with by all the teachers involved. It was agreed to tackle specific assignments from other thematic areas during the year and to do so in consultation with each other. To begin with, CDT would work with home economics on 'Getting Around' and information technology would link with art and design to undertake 'Fantastic Inventions'. Home economics, alone, could also run 'Fit for the Job', and art and design could undertake 'It's not What you Say'. As the year progressed, areas not being adequately covered by the cross-curricular activities would be identified and a choice of special assignments offered. The programme as a whole seemed to offer a good range of contexts and outcomes and would begin to break down the perception of the main subjects as discrete areas.

The planning group then turned their attention to what the pupils might then go on to undertake in the following year. They noticed that all the main topics had been covered, with the exception of 'Work, Rest and Play', although some had only been briefly introduced, suggesting the use of a commercial context for a major cross-curricular project. A guided choice of further, perhaps more specialised, assignments running at the same time might help pupils develop their particular interests and skills.

Towards the end of their discussion, however, whilst acknowledging that they were beginning to get a better sense of their ultimate goal, the planners realised that their ideas were much too ambitious for an initial stage of implementation. They therefore decided to propose keeping the initial 'Shipwrecked' project, but only involving three members of the design and technology staff who were particularly interested, and a geography and an English teacher. It was also thought easier to contain the project within the normal timetable pattern of two double periods a week. They also decided to retain the 'Village-study' project, still following the existing structure, but this time being more speculative. It was also felt that the suspended timetable at the end of the year should still go ahead as a high priority, involving as many staff in the school as possible, with the choice of final theme being established and agreed by those who participated.

Assessment in design and technological education

The Task Group on Assessment and Testing (TGAT) have suggested that 'Assessment is at the heart of the process of promoting children's learning'. In your group discuss the extent to which you agree or disagree with this statement.

In our age of 'accountability', the need for regular and rigorous assessment of performance has become increasingly necessary. A great deal of published material is already available on testing and profiling approaches and methodologies in general. This section briefly identifies some of the central issues involved in the formal recording and assessment of design and technological activities – issues which are likely to be the most influential of all in determining the eventual nature and success of future developments.

Assessment in schools serves a number of related, but subtly different purposes. First, there is the evaluation of a pupil's achievement and progress made by the teacher as a formative, diagnostic indicator of particular strengths and weaknesses, for the purposes of directing subsequent tasks at an appropriate level. There is also the usually more formal summative assessment, often used as the basis for a public statement of attainment of a particular level of achievement, and which is controlled by an external agency of some sort. It is tempting to allow the structure of the formal assessment to lead the diagnostic procedures, but it should be realised that this is not always appropriate. Finally, though not the concern of this session, there are also the processes of evaluative analysis of how well the performance of the teacher, the effectiveness of a programme of study and/or the school are measuring up to national standards.

Formal assessment in design and technological education is particularly difficult because of the inherent lack of uniformity between individual pupils of the same age tackling individual assignments in individual ways. To present test activities which prescribe particular processes, time-scales or types of outcome is not only contrary to the nature of designing, but penalises children who do not happen to be familiar with or interested in the topic, or happen to think and act in a certain way. Seen in this way, short-term, isolated 'tests' are unlikely to reveal very much of the true capability of each pupil: the fluidity and extended time-scale of the processes of designing, which allows the mind to begin to understand and unconsciously dwell on the complex inter-relationships of the elements of the problem, is critical.

An 'objective' numerical marking system is also clearly inappropriate in circumstances where there are no right or wrong answers and no directly comparable standards. Dividing a project into linear and equally marked process-based stages has its drawbacks too, because for different pupils, different processes and end-products will have been proportionally more or less demanding across the process as a whole. Under such circumstances it is more appropriate to assess the development and achievement of pupils on the basis of a wide range of assignments, each of which has provided opportunities to emphasise the development of both strengths and weaknesses in particular aspects of the process as a whole.

The need for standardisation of formal, external assessment procedures is particularly important, and depends on the quality of the ability of external assessors and moderators to identify the level of attainment achieved in contexts and outcomes in which they may or may not be particularly experienced.

To enable assessment of cognitive processes it is essential for children to become aware of the need to supply the necessary **evidence** of their developmental processes of thought and action. This entails getting into the habit of recording ideas in a permanent form if imaginative possibilities and carefully considered decisions are not to be lost. When asked to account for courses of action they have followed, pupils are often able to provide verbal descriptions which reveal sound, perceptive and ingenious thinking, and it is precisely these ideas which they need to be encouraged to record. Often the evidence will be in visual rather than verbal form. Ideally such documentation should be undertaken as part of the developmental process, but on occasion it might be retrospective. It must, however, also be realised that many good ideas are not the result of conscious, analytic and structured processes, and so spontaneity and intuitiveness should also be valued. The process of documentation should not therefore be over-emphasised, and it should be necessary only for pupils to clearly demonstrate depth and quality of thought and action in a proportion or even parts of their assignments undertaken during a given year.

Discuss the extent to which the provision of rigorous analytic evidence of thought and action might limit the development of confidence in intuitive approaches and of creative potential. Try to identify specific previous tasks which have placed too much or too little emphasis on documentation.

Refer to the intended formal, external assessment criteria and procedures for design and technological-related activity in the National Curriculum. To what extent do they conform to or contradict the statements made above?

Internal assessment/profiling

Devising an effective internal assessment/profiling system to monitor the progress of each pupil is going to be itself a complex design activity which will take considerable development and testing. In most schools the scheme will probably also have to be considered as part of a larger whole-school profile system.

By the end of each key stage teachers will need to have ensured that pupils have covered:
- a broad enough range of contexts
- each area of the programmes of study to the appropriate level
- a broad enough range of outcomes.

This will require a continual and cumulative system of record-keeping and indication of performance for each individual pupil – a highly time-consuming task which should not be underestimated. Ideally the pupils should participate in both the recording and assessment of progress as much as possible. Again, each school will need to devise its own particular approach.

Attempt to devise an integrated assessment/profile/storage of work system for design and technological activity in your school. You will need to consider the following:
- What aspects of design and technological activity, such as the adequate coverage of areas of knowledge, experience of using particular tools and materials etc. will need to be covered?
- How often will the various forms be used?
- To what extent would your proposals form an appropriate component of your school profiling system?
- What are the practical administrative implications of your proposed system?
- How much will it cost to implement?
- Where will everything be stored?

To complete successfully, this activity would take a co-ordinating group several working days to produce the basis of a trial package. As a possible starting point, the following case study is a brief description of part of an internal project record and assessment scheme which has been successfully tried and tested across the 11 to 14 age-range undertaking cross-curricular design and technological activities. The **Project Summary/Record** form (p. 95) may be photocopied free of charge if wished, provided the source acknowledgement at the bottom is not deleted.

Case study

At the end of every major assignment or sequence of related activities, pupils should individually write a summary of the work they have done, outlining the investigative methods and developmental stages which have been used. A description of the nature of the final realisation should be provided, possibly in the form of a sketch or diagram on the back of the sheet. They should then attempt an evaluation of their own work, with particular reference to the process as well as the quality of the end-product. Older pupils may well need to continue on the reverse. It is suggested that pupils use the 'prompt' questions provided on page 8 of *Introducing Design*.

The tutor then adds a comment, which ideally has been discussed and negotiated with the pupil, and the forms should then be collated and retained. As far as possible the work of the pupils is also retained. A3 and A4 2D work is kept in individual pocket files which are updated every year. Larger 2D work is kept in plan-chest drawers, and 3D items in storerooms.

Design and technological education issues

There are many problems and potential difficulties to explore, understand and resolve in the implementation of design and technology in schools, and no simple answers. This section, therefore, identifies a selection of some of the central issues involved and aims to raise awareness and promote discussion, rather than to provide instant solutions.

Teaching for profit

The press reports covering the publication of the Consultative Report in June 1989 presented an emphasis on a 'teaching for profit' approach through product design and 'young enterprise' business education. Whilst fully supporting the need for industry and commerce to make a greater contribution to education, it is important that teachers lead and closely monitor school-industry links to ensure that broad educational goals are achieved alongside the increased awareness of the world of work and business skills. A developing industry/school partnership needs to be seen as a two-way process in which businesses themselves become more aware of the capabilities of school-leavers and the ways in which their employees can continue to learn after they have left school.

Just as industry aims to produce products, services and profits, teachers are in the business of producing people: using the role of a professional designer must be seen as a vehicle for learning, and the constraints and demands of the specialised and commercial values of the 'real world' frequently need to be modified and distilled if they are to enable children to receive a sufficiently broad and balanced education (and, for that matter, to cover the breadth of the required programmes of study adequately).

To what extent will it be possible to resolve the subtle differences of aims and objectives when undertaking educational activity which is closely linked to industrial and commercial practices?

Teaching without resources

Whilst financial provision for implementing design and technology might well be higher than for many other National Curriculum subjects, it is never likely to be enough. Although extensive re-equipping and refurbishing of accommodation

What does your house look like?
(p. 64)
Legoids (p. 86)

Elevations describe the vertical planes of objects (their fronts, sides and backs), and reveal arrangements of components and their surroundings, using a similar imaginary two-dimensional viewpoint.

Listening in (2) (p. 48)

Orthographic projection is the term used to describe the use of measured plans and elevations on one drawing. When read together they can provide all the technical information necessary to describe a three-dimensional object accurately.

General assembly drawing (sometimes described as a **production** or **workshop drawing**) is an orthographic projection of an assembled object with overall dimensions, descriptions of materials to be used and numbered component parts. Separate detailed, measured drawings in orthographic projection are then provided for each component together with clear assembly instructions.

Isometric projections (30°) provide a quick and easy method of showing how an object will look in three dimensions.

See section symbols (p. 6)
My house (3) (p. 66)

Axonometric drawings (45°) are usually used for drawings of spaces or buildings. They have an advantage over isometrics in that circular forms are easier to construct.

Terminus (2) (p. 83)

Perspective drawings give the most realistic illusion of depth, and are more visually understandable. In sketch form one- and two-point perspectives are fairly easy to draw, but three-point and accurate measured perspectives are difficult and time-consuming to get right.

Listening in (5) (p. 51)

Exploded views of a three-dimensional drawing of an object can be effective in showing the way in which various components fit together.

Cross-sections are made from plans or elevations as if a slice has been cut through part or all of an object or structure.

Cut-aways are similar to cross-sections, with the cut-away removing the outer portions of an object or enclosed space in order to reveal more information about its interior.

Rendering is the process of applying colour, texture, tonal shading, shadows and reflections to a drawing in order to give greater visual impact and realism by providing further information about the look and feel of the surfaces of materials, to make objects look more solid, to give a greater illusion of depth, and to emphasise or code various components.

Visual devices are used to make the graphic presentation of ideas more lively so as to attract attention and sustain interest. Lines, blocks of colours, overlays, photomontages, collages, etc., can help achieve this, together with the possible use of cartoons, storyboards, animatics and low-relief models.

Everyday objectivity (p. 39)
Listening in (3) (p. 49)
Increasing speed (p. 87)
Sandwich survey (p. 103)

Graphs and charts are effective for representing statistical data or for the comparison of related information. Adding colour and other pictorial images can make the graph or chart considerably more interesting and understandable.

Overlays. Images drawn on to a transparent material and placed over a related image, can provide a highly effective 'before' and 'after' stage by stage statement, or can enable the effect of various alternatives to be easily compared. They also encourage valuable 'user participation'.

Paintings/drawings/prints in some situations might be appropriate forms of realisations, providing they have been developed through the use of a design-related process, and are in response to the given context or situation.

The domestic help (p. 55)

Cartoons/storyboards and animatics. A cartoon sequence is a very lively and dynamic way of presenting an idea through the use of humour and exaggeration: difficult concepts can often be communicated very concisely in this way. A storyboard, a timed series of related visuals, spoken words and/or music, is needed in the planning of each shot and sequence of a proposed film or video sequence. An animatic is where the drawn illustrations on the storyboard are shot in sequence, and the sound added, giving a realistic effect of the proposed film or video.

Lettering (typography). There are many different styles of lettering which can be used or adapted for titles. Legibility should be a prime consideration in striving for a balance between style, height and thickness of letter form. Letter stencils are rarely effective as they offer little choice.

Layout. In most 'public' situations a selection of the above two-dimensional graphic techniques would be formally presented on sheets of card, or as pages of a smaller-scale report of some sort. A series of display panels or pages might each utilise a variety of such techniques, with the layout visually related by co-ordinated grid layouts, colours and typefaces. Such devices can serve a number of important purposes:
- to break up large areas of blank space
- to add visual style, or character
- to help unify the series of display panels or pages.

A series of display panels or presentation sheets might form a 'portfolio', or be presented as an exhibition of some sort. Meanwhile at a 'technical' level, drawings are commonly presented on A1 sheets of drafting (tracing) paper, or as 'die-line' or 'diazo' prints. A good photocopier with enlargement and reduction facilities can be most useful in the production of graphic work, as it facilitates paste-ups and improved sizing of line-drawings. Where available, access to a Pagemaker word-processing computer system to produce graphic work can be a highly effective tool, particularly when matched by a laser printer. Although expensive at present, such items are, however, likely to become common place within the next five years.

Other forms of presentation

In some 'public' situations, other forms of presentation might be appropriate.

Audio-tape could be used to communicate ideas for material which might be broadcast, or for musical compositions. A co-ordinated tape-slide presentation can be very effective if done properly. **Film** is another possibility, but is much more expensive and difficult for younger pupils to control successfully. **Video-tape**, however, is cheap and relatively simple to use if a camera and recorder are available. A domestic model is quite adequate, and simple editing is possible if two recorders can be linked together. Most images are considerably enhanced by the addition of a musical sound-track which can usually be easily over-dubbed.

Computer-generated images have increasing potential for attracting attention and stimulating interest, largely because of the bright colours which are produced and the possibilities for animation. It is often possible to edit computer-generated images directly into video-tape sequences.

Local issues (p. 33)
Human factors (p. 35)
Job centre (p. 54)
Person to person (p. 74)
Holiday exchange (p. 84)
Roboritual (p. 92)

Performance (drama, movement, costume, music, etc.) is also a highly effective means of getting a message across, though it takes a great deal of preparation and usually involves a team of people working together. In certain situations, however, the 'performance' might simply be the designer having to personally present his ideas, possibly by introducing and talking through a series of drawings and models. It is valuable to perceive this situation as a performance, paying attention to delivery and appearance, and carefully co-ordinating speech with visual illustrations.

An important part of such a presentation can be the messages transmitted, usually unconsciously, through what is called **body language**. The way a person sits, the gestures and facial expressions which are made and the way in which clothes are worn all say a great deal. To a certain extent it is possible to manipulate situations so that clients will feel more relaxed and open, confrontations can be avoided, authority can be retained, confidence generated, etc.

Creative writing, such as a piece of prose, poetry or song-lyric will in some circumstances be an appropriate form of realisation, but generally within the context of a broader-based presentation, such as an illustrated children's book, a play, or perhaps the copy for an advertisement. Another possibility might be the production of an extended critical review of an existing product, place or communication.

Formal writing techniques are frequently used for research and project development reports. The style should not be personal (e.g. 'it was decided...' rather than 'I decided') and there are various structures which are commonly used (for example: summary, introduction, research method, data, findings, evaluation, conclusion, further development, notes, sources, appendix, index). There are also conventions used for references to illustrations and written sources, and systems for numbering paragraphs.

Stages of development

3D constructions

Assignments which involve a broad range of mainly 2D realisation/presentation techniques:

The initial construction of appearance-models can be very straightforward, and provides an ideal opportunity to introduce young pupils to basic workshop skills of cutting, shaping and simple joining of a wide range of materials. Paper and card can be most effectively used, and children are usually very familiar with their working properties. Pupils should have the opportunity to construct 'block' models (e.g. in 'Listening in') where material is initially removed. A high standard of detailing and finish is needed, which, with guidance, most pupils can achieve. As pupils become more experienced, more complex and durable structures constructed to a more accurate scale can be expected. Quite sophisticated card models can be achieved. Most senior pupils should be quite capable of producing highly realistic models.

2D graphic work and other forms of realisation

Most eleven-year-olds can draw maps and plans of places and spaces, and this can usually be extended into the idea of a plan and elevation of an object and, with practice, of an orthographic projection, supported by overall dimensioning. During the first two years isometrics and axonometrics can also be introduced: perspectives will prove difficult for most, though some pupils will be able to manage simple constructions. A wide range of ability to render effectively (i.e. apply and control a range of graphic media) can usually be observed at this level, and pupils need to be actively encouraged to experiment with mixing different pencils, pens, paints, etc., in order to represent different textured and coloured surfaces. Visual devices are rarely utilised at this stage, particularly when presenting graphs and charts. Pupils are, however, becoming more aware of their potential, as they are now widely used in magazines, advertising and packaging aimed at this age. Many children can produce good cartoon work.

The layout of text and illustrations on a final presentation sheet or panel needs considerable emphasis and explanation. Once the basic concepts have been grasped this does not prove to be difficult. Pupils need to be made aware of decisions about lettering styles and size. A proportion of projects undertaken during a year should be presented as a formal report. With appropriate preparation, pupils are generally good at performance activities, particularly if working in a small group. Standards of formal and creative verbal expression are also usually quite high in comparison to visual and spatial representational skills.

Perhaps the key weakness in the development of skills is in the ability to use appropriate mixtures of visual and verbal techniques. There is a tendency for pupils to produce a single drawing and provide no written explanation, or to write an extended piece of prose and add an illustration at the end, rather as an afterthought. Children need to have the opportunity to have the freedom of choice of realisation and presentation media, and be encouraged to think carefully about what they need to communicate, and then to consider the best ways of communicating that information. The effectiveness of their decisions can be evaluated through 'public' presentation sessions to either the rest of the group or, as part of an exhibition, to the school.

Development in the third and fourth years is largely a matter of revision and increased sophistication. Pupils should be capable of producing accurate, scaled presentation and workshop drawings of simple objects. Practice in freehand three-dimensional sketching is probably more important than the production of measured drawings, which can be time-consuming. Preparation is needed to illustrate a more detailed verbal account with co-ordinated references to visual material.

Fifth and sixth formers should be proficient in the full range and formality of realisation and presentation techniques as appropriate and will often achieve very high standards, though weaker pupils will often revert to using a very limited range of techniques.

Everyday Objects
Design: Processes and Products
(T263 Units 2-4)
Brown, S
The Open University, 1983

Evaluation

Throughout the process of identifying and solving problems pupils are constantly assessing and evaluating:
- the merits and shortcomings of existing solutions
- the potential value of their design ideas as they progress towards the proposal of a solution
- their own strengths and weaknesses of personal performance.

In a sequential design-process it is common to emphasise evaluation as the last stage: in practice it forms a dimension of the techniques of investigation, modelling and realisation of ideas. An enhanced critical vocabulary enables a far more effective evaluation to take place.

As well as deliberately aiming to increase pupils' word-power through activities involving the description and evaluation of existing products, places and communications, providing 'prompt' questions is perhaps the best way to develop the capacity to evaluate. A selection of such questions is provided on page 8 of *Introducing Design*. It is important to use them more as a checklist, and responses need to be in the form of complete sentences. Younger pupils in particular need to be guided away from simplistic yes- or no-type answers. Obviously not all the questions are relevant to every stage of every project and every pupil, so they need to be selected as appropriate. Pupils should be encouraged to refer to them frequently during the progress of an assignment, and reminded that they will help originate appropriate diary entries, as well as the final evaluation. Children also need to be reminded to aim to include a mixture of good and bad points, and when analysing existing artefacts, systems and environments to take into account the differing needs of others.

Stages of development

Although first and second year pupils are often aware of the overall standard of existing products, places and communications, and of their own progress and achievements, their ability to externalise and express their evaluation is often rather minimal, though this can be notably improved by use of a checklist and reference to a wordlist. During these early stages the quality of dialogue with the teacher is particularly important. With prompting, good descriptive work is usually possible, though qualitative comments remain generally unsophisticated.

It is not until the third year that some students begin to produce really perceptive comments, though 'prompt' questions still remain helpful. Only in the fifth and sixth form does the ability to evaluate effectively seem to mature, with pupils finally becoming perceptive and articulate in their statements. Most students are well aware of the shortcomings of their own work, and if anything tend to be over-critical.

Planning and organisation

Design Project Guide
Man-made Futures, Unit 12
Roy, R
Open University Press, 1975

Systems, Management and Change
Carter, Martin, Mayblin and Munday
Harper & Row/Open University,
1985

The skilful planning and organisation of actions and resources is essential to successful design activity. As with evaluation, it forms a dimension of each of the investigation/development/realisation skills. Schoolchildren are used to having their daily lives organised for them and have often had little practice in using their own initiative and planning ahead.

The ability to 'make things happen' involves developing a sense of an overall strategy (a framework of intended actions), followed by a series of shorter-term tactical decisions to help movement in the appropriate direction through the framework. This involves the careful management of the resources which are available:

- time (how much can be realistically achieved?)
- information (is any essential information easily available?)
- materials (are the necessary materials obtainable?)
- tools (are the necessary tools readily available?)
- finance (is the anticipated cost of design development acceptable?)
- ability (are the various levels of demand of the development process appropriate to the capabilities of the problem solver?)

Effective action also requires the organisation of others in the sense of being able to obtain the willing and helpful assistance of others, particularly when working as part of a team. Pupils need to consider:

- whose assistance would be useful
- why the person should be interested in providing assistance
- how he or she should be approached.

In most assignments the teacher is likely to establish the overall strategy, setting firm deadlines for the completion of the whole task, and probably several of the intermediate stages. Pupils do need to be given increasing responsibility for planning and organising their work, however. They should be encouraged to think about:

- which actions will need to be done first, and which can be left till later
- when all the research needs to be complete
- when developmental stages will need to begin
- when the final realisation stages need to be started and completed.

A number of team-based projects need to be set during each year to encourage the growth of collaborative skills, something which pupils find difficult. A good approach is to set team projects which allow a number of tasks to be shared out amongst the members, so that the contribution of each individual can be more precisely identified. Keeping an individual diary of the progress of the project is also essential in group work.

One of the most important aspects of learning how to plan and organise is to become able to deal with unexpected developments, as opposed to giving up when things go wrong. Completing a weekly **Project Schedule** (p. 96) helps ensure that pupils have an overall view of the available time and have planned ahead. At the end of each week there should be a brief account of what was actually achieved in relation to the targets set, and subsequent 'intended actions' can then be modified as necessary. The schedule sheet is similar to, but not to be confused with, the project diary, as it is much less detailed and reflective. Plotting the intended plan of action graphically (in some form of flow diagram) can be helpful.

Stages of development

Although younger secondary school children need well-structured assignments, it is important at an early stage to give them experience of self-organisation. Setting two or more short tasks concurrently, and inviting pupils to decide on which to start and complete first is one approach: this should be applied to investigative, developmental and realisation activities. Keeping to firm deadlines for completing stages of work is important, though this needs to be balanced with a less rigorous approach on occasion when it is considered that some extra time might produce more worthwhile results.

Some projects at this stage should be team-based, which younger pupils always seem keen on, but find difficult to manage. All too often one member of the group does all the work which is copied up by the others, so such activities need very careful monitoring. Short-term tasks are the most effective, as often are those involving the presentation of a performance.

Third and fourth years are capable of planning and organising their work over longer periods of time (on average about three weeks) and, when motivated, using their initiative to deal with unexpected problems. Several research and developmental activities can be set at the same time with a stated completion date. Team projects can be very successful, depending on the particular make-up of the group.

Fifth and sixth formers often continue to find the planning and organisation of work a problem. Although they should be set increasingly longer-term projects (balanced by a number of short-term assignments) they cannot be relied on to work to schedule. Indeed the main role of a tutor at this level is often to simply ensure that work is up to date, and is meeting the proportional requirements of the examination syllabus. Group projects continue to cause difficulties, as larger teams of pupils often find it hard to meet and work together outside formal lesson times. Most examination syllabuses, whilst aiming to encourage collaborative work, do little to facilitate it in their assessment systems: well defined individual targets and detailed diary work are the best approach to group activities. Occasionally, however, two or three pupils do form an effective working relationship which can be advantageously developed further. Establishing teams from across the school age range can be an interesting exercise: older pupils often work better with first or second years than with each other.

Overall approach

In contrast to the more general nature of the previous sessions, this one is directly related to the assignments presented in *Introducing Design*. The overall approach to the assignments in *Introducing Design* is thematic: pupils moving up from primary school will find this reassuringly familiar. Each main technologically-related theme contains an introduction and a series of exploratory mini-assignments which, if required, could be realised within a double lesson, although most could be extended over several sessions and homeworks. Subsequent pages then present the framework for an extended project which could occupy pupils for up to half the school year, and conclude with suggestions for other related assignments, each with a selection of starting questions.

Many of the activities can be undertaken by pupils individually or working in teams. Each assignment is firmly placed in a context – some of which are imaginary, some within the existing personal experience of the pupils, and others for which further primary and secondary information will be essential. Each thematic section includes a number of discussion issues which could be used to promote consideration of social implications and human values.

In some situations the book as a whole could be used to form the basic structure of a three year programme of cross-curricular activity. More generally, however, it can be used as a supplement to existing work, and as stimulus of the development of new projects, tailored to fit the requirements of particular groups of pupils and classroom circumstances. To facilitate this each single- and double-page spread has, wherever possible, been designed to stand on its own. The assignments are of particular relevance to art and design, CDT, home economics and business education, and also to drama, media studies and science. They could, therefore, provide a valuable aid to linking and co-ordinating such areas together in the National Curriculum.

Details of the relevant specific areas of knowledge relating to the use of tools, components and the working properties of materials have not been included: this information will be found to be well-documented in existing subject-based publications.

Introducing Design is organised into two main sections. The first includes the key **design skills** which, in different mixtures, will be needed for all the activities and assignments. The **assessment checklists** provide a means of ensuring that individual pupils are gaining a broad enough experience of the skills.

The second section presents the broadest possible range of assignments based on ten design and technological themes which relate to the familiar everyday experiences and concerns of children – shelter, community, food, clothing, transport, information, everyday objects, fair exchange, work, rest and play, and design and society.

Shipwrecked, the first major assignment introduces all the themes by placing the pupils on a remote desert island and inviting them to work out how they are going to survive without the assistance of modern technology. Having identified and considered their most basic survival needs, pupils are rescued and then re-presented with the themes and, through subsequent assignments, discover how design and technology has increasingly come to enhance their survival, and speculate on the nature and desirability of the likely future interaction between people and machines and devices.

With this in mind the final theme, **Design and society**, asks pupils to reflect on the survival needs of their society and of Spaceship Earth as a whole, providing an appropriate concluding reflection of the assignments they have undertaken.

Assignment briefings

Because of the open-ended nature of the projects in *Introducing Design* it would be both inappropriate and impossible to provide notes for each assignment which specified in detail the resources to be prepared, exactly how long each activity should last, and what the 'right' answer would be. Instead, therefore, the following notes are intended to reveal more about the way in which pupils are likely to respond, indicating aspects of the activities they are likely to find easy or difficult. There are also suggestions for ways of extending the assignments which help give an indication of how design projects are generally formed and developed. From such an awareness it should be possible for you to begin to be able to generate and deliver further starting points which are uniquely suited to the particular requirements of your school, classroom, pupils, and yourself.

As a very rough guide to assist with initial planning, **activity** assignments can be undertaken in a double lesson (i.e. 60 to 90 minutes) and perhaps completed at home during the week. Most **assignments** are generally intended to last between two and five double lessons. **Major assignments** are likely to occupy at least six double lessons, though will frequently need up to twelve sessions.

At this initial stage it is advisable to read through the whole text for this session, as many of the individual project notes contain comments and ideas which could be appropriately applied to other assignments.

Page numbers throughout this session refer to *Introducing Design*.

As you read through the notes for each assignment decide for which level in your school you feel it is most appropriate. Discuss how it might be simplified for use at a lower level, or developed for use at a higher level.

For each assignment, make a note of the specific areas of knowledge which could be covered.

Introduction (page 4)

These pages form an important introductory session in which the concepts which underlie the whole book are outlined to the pupils. In most situations it is perhaps worth reading through these pages formally with a group, elaborating the key points by providing further examples and inviting class contributions and discussion. It should be remembered that pupils may find it valuable to review these introductory pages at a later stage in the course, with the hindsight of the experience of having undertaken a selection of the assignments.

Design skills (page 7)

Beyond perhaps a passing reference and/or quick read through, it is not recommended that each design skill be formally presented at the very start of any course. Pupils are understandably keen to get going, and it is important not to give the initial impression that the work is going to be all book-based and teacher-led. Instead, the design skills are best introduced in the context of a longer-term project, and pupils should be frequently reminded that they are there for later reference during any project which is being undertaken: indeed, such practice should be explicitly encouraged throughout the course, and in particular when pupils are evaluating their own progress. The Assessment Checklist boxes emphasise the need to provide clear evidence of the application of the design skills.

If, however, the formal introduction of the design skills is considered desirable outside the context of an assignment, a series of isolated short-term exercises could be devised to help give some sense of context. Do try to ensure, however, that each skill does not become perceived as separate from the others, and, as such, part of a rigid linear sequence.

Shipwrecked (page 18)

Survival/Rescue (pages 18 to 25)

This extended introductory assignment is specifically intended as an opportunity to demonstrate to pupils the extent to which we have all become dependent on modern technology for our survival. As well as providing practical everyday problems to be solved, it places them in the context of the emotional needs of being castaway. The project also introduces the cross-curricular nature of design and technological activity, and although it does not have to be the first theme to be undertaken, it certainly effectively establishes the 'whole', after which the various assignments in the rest of the course will make more sense.

The project could be delivered in one of a number of different ways:
- a short intensive programme during which part, or all, of the normal timetable is suspended
- following a general introductory session, several subject areas combine, or each deals with different topics
- spread across a regular 'cross-curricular' slot on the timetable.

The extent to which the work should be teacher-led is also variable, and perhaps ideally pupils should experience a mixture of approaches. The project always seems to manage to create a great deal of involvement, enthusiasm and excitement so it is quite possible, and indeed an ideal opportunity, for staff to 'let go' and give the pupils a free choice of direction, providing their ideas are documented and gently guided, and fit broadly into one or more of the topic headings. Alternatively, however, a specific problem could be identified and directed research and development undertaken by the whole class. Somewhere between these two extremes would be the provision of some choice of topic and problem combined with a number of specific activities and time-scales, but always with the opportunity for pupils to make their own suggestions for possible further directions.

Although all the key topic areas should be covered, particular emphasis could of course be given to some at the expense of others. Most pupils in the upper-primary and secondary age ranges will be experienced enough to make some attempt to solve the problems posed and realise their ideas through written statements, drawings and/or simple models. There are plenty of opportunities to introduce each of the basic design skills informally.

The ocean liner **imagination** sequence is undoubtedly presented most effectively as an improvised drama situation. With an experienced teacher at the helm, sixty or so pupils can easily be organised into various role-playing situations, even if they have had little previous drama experience. The adventure can be started at an earlier point – packing suitcases (what would you take?), saying goodbye at the station / airport, writing home and so on. The sight of an ocean liner with a full complement of crew and passengers steaming majestically down the school hall is not to be missed! On a given cue, participants should react to the explosion and stay in role as everyone escapes from the sinking ship.

A highly effective (though perhaps rather ambitious) conclusion to this stage is to find a small classroom in the school which can be blacked-out, and fill it as far as possible with sand, adding the actual objects found on the beach (or cards with drawings or the names of the objects on). Slides of the sea and a desert island can be projected onto screens, and pupils then pass through the room in pairs or small groups as if struggling up the sea-shore, and are asked to retrieve one or more items. Ideally the items listed on page 19 should all be actually available for inspection and possible use: a modified list could be substituted if necessary. It is not, however, essential for them all to be physically available as they are all familiar objects which can be easily represented in drawing or model form. Pupils frequently ask questions such as 'how long is the coil of rope?', and such decisions must be left to the discretion of the teacher at that particular moment in the development of the project (and the individual child). A few pupils might well point out that because there is hardly any paper on the island they wouldn't be able to draw and write about their ideas, but most are happy to accept the artificiality of the situation without questioning it.

Another activity which can be undertaken before tackling the main projects is the exploration of the island. Given its latitude and longitude (taken from the navigation map on page 17), more information can be discovered about the climate and natural resources. An imaginary terrain can be plotted and mapped out, and even sculpted as a small-scale relief model.

Turning to the individual themes, initially a broad overview is valuable, followed by more detailed work. Some activities might be teacher-led, whilst others are directed entirely by pupils. Children need to be encouraged to ask questions whilst considering the possible consequences of their ideas. For example, if the mirror is to be used for signalling:
● How will it be held?
● Where will it be safely kept?
● How can that place be marked?
This in turn should lead to the development of ideas and their final realisation.

The need for effective communication of ideas is reinforced by the requirement on page 19 that other survivors may want to use the tools and materials for different purposes, so that 'you will always need to make out a very good case to include them in any of your plans'. For more complex items the equivalent of working drawings should be made to explain in detail how they would be constructed. Pupils might imagine that they have to present each of their proposals to everyone on the island so that it can be decided which plans should be implemented. The checklist questions at the top of page 21 will help pupils structure their presentation.

A high percentage of the work can be undertaken by small teams (two to four), though it is important for pupils to record their own documentation. An illustrated diary, imaginatively written, and compiled as a separate document from the developmental work, forms an effective way of identifying the work of the individual, and tying the whole 'adventure' together.

A surprising amount of potential material is to be found within this project. The activities suggested in the text represent a small proportion of the many problems and issues which can arise, and sometimes limits will need to be imposed.

Rescue provides a appropriate conclusion to the project, inviting pupils to consider comparisons of the simple quality of life on the desert island with the advantages and disadvantages of the high-technology world of today. A group debate might reveal some interesting opinions and attitudes towards life expectations. How many would actually vote to stay on the island?

Media event provides an added dimension in its exploration and questioning of the role and ethics of the press. How far should they go to 'sell' the story? A 'Newspaper' computer software package might be effectively utilised here. Meanwhile **Exhibition** is an ideal opportunity for pupils to mount a display of cross-curricular work in design and technology for presentation to staff, parents, governors, etc.

Everyday products, places and communications (page 26)

In terms of the sequence of the book this activity is intended as an important link between **Shipwrecked** and the subsequent topics. It could be covered at some other time, however, and makes a useful alternative introductory project if **Shipwrecked** is not being undertaken at the start of a course. The various lists which are generated form a useful personal resource of common artefacts which pupils have at home: indeed several assignments specifically refer back to the lists as starting points.

Pupils usually find little difficulty identifying the difference between **products** and **places**, but **communications** sometimes cause confusion. A television set, for example, is actually a product, and it is the signal (the picture and sound) which is the communication. A book is a product, the words and the book jacket, communications. Some other artefacts will cause difficulties because they could fit into more than one category, and of course in reality nothing is ever truly two-dimensional. After pupils have been compiling their own lists for a while it can be effective to stimulate broader thinking by suggesting that they try and think of the smallest and largest, highest and lowest, newest and oldest examples that they have at home.

In the final diagram the visual concept of drawing just enough of each item to make it recognisable is quite sophisticated and some pupils may find this difficult. The idea of letting part of the image break the boundary of the circle is a frequently used graphic device, but one which children would not normally think of using. Using the circle as part of the picture (as with the watch) is another simple concept which has to be directly encouraged. This exercise often provides an early indication of which pupils find difficulties with thinking visually, and/or controlling the media. Allow at least 30 minutes for compiling the lists, around an hour for preparation of the A3 sheet, and a further hour for its completion.

Community (page 28)

Most people need a place to relate to – somewhere they can feel comfortable, and where they are familiar with its geography, institutions and other inhabitants. A community is a highly complicated system – a unique mixture of people, places and spaces, and communications, all in some way dependent on each other. The spatial and visual way in which the various components – its roads, shops, houses, businesses, public spaces, parks, etc. – are arranged can exert a great deal of influence on the way in which people feel and behave.

Sources of further information

Royal Institute of British Architects
66 Portland Place
London W1N 4AD (071-580 5533)

Royal Town Planning Institute,
26 Portland Place
London W1N 4BE (071-580 2436)

Bibliography

Townscape
Cullen, G
Architectural Press, 1961

Cities with a Future
Baynes, K
Channel 4/The Design Council, 1987

The Pattern Language
Alexander, C
Oxford University Press, 1977

Cities Fit to Live in
Sherman, B
Channel 4, 1988

*Art and the Built Environment:
A Teacher's Approach*
Adams and Ward
Longman, 1982

*Art and the Built Environment:
Study Activities*
Adams and Baynes
Longman, 1982

Townscape Study Sheets
Scoffham and Shepard
RIBA/Canterbury Urban Studies
Centre

*Transformations: Process and
Theory*
Nelson, D
City Building Programs, 1984

How to Play the Environment Game
Crosby, T
Penguin, 1973

Responsive Environments
Bently, Alcock, Murrain, McGlynn,
Smith
Architectural Press, 1985

*Communities, Planning and
Participation*
Design: Processes and Products
(T263, Units 14-15)
Boyle, G
The Open University, 1983

Understanding our Community
Picton, M
Blackie, 1986

Many modern cities are based on the the prime requirements of efficiency of movement and land values. Mass housing estates have no shopping or leisure facilities, shopping precincts are deserted at night and are open to vandalism. Public transport systems have become unreliable, infrequent and expensive, leaving many people isolated and lonely. A strong sense of community is, however, one of the most important elements in the growth of a secure, comfortable and productive lifestyle, particularly in a society which values individual achievement so highly. All children live in or belong to a community of some sort, though they may not realise or value it, and need to be encouraged to recognise the qualities which contribute to the growth of a successful community, and to understand that if they contribute to it in some way, it will in turn support them.

Architects' and planners' attempts to pre-plan communities have rarely worked well. The most successful communities seem to grow naturally, around a particular neighbourhood, hospital, school or church perhaps, and the best planning schemes recognise this and attempt to facilitate growth from within.

Liaison with local community groups, social services and county planning officers is often relatively easy to arrange, and introductory speakers, local information, planning briefs, etc., are readily available.

Work under the heading of 'Environmental Education' will obviously be closely connected with this theme, though it needs to be approached from a cross-curricular perspective.

Environmental evaluation (page 29)

It is often best to begin an assignment like this with a short introductory session evaluating the school grounds (see also **Schoolscapes**). As with most evaluation exercises, pupils tend to rely too heavily on description as they find it more difficult to express critical responses. It is also important to emphasise that sketches can be very diagrammatic, and should be annotated where possible – works of 'art' are not expected.

A high street, or even a small row of shops, within easy reach of the school is an excellent location to take a group out to: small villages or farmyards are other good possibilities. A housing estate is more demanding to tackle, but nonetheless can produce much valuable material. Giving each child a specific location within the site can be a good idea. Alternatively the assignment can be tackled on an individual basis and children asked to identify a site based within easy access of their home. Sketches and notes can be made during the week and neatly presented in class. A much wider variety of location becomes possible, and a historical research element can be effectively introduced, although detailed studies of historic buildings, with no comment on the present, or speculation about the future, should be avoided.

In both situations it is advisable, particularly with younger and/or less experienced pupils, to set some fairly specific tasks – particular observation and drawing work. Final presentation can be as simple or complex as desired, from an A3 sheet or 8 page booklet, to a tape-slide or video sequence. The assignment could also be further developed through a 'making proposals for change' approach, possibly culminating in a public presentation of drawings and models to the local community for their comments.

Schoolscapes (page 30)

Much of the material for these assignments has been based on the 'Learning through Landscapes' project. Project work can be appropriately evaluated by mounting a display and obtaining responses from the school community as a whole to the proposed changes or events. It is frequently possible to implement some of the less ambitious ideas which are generated. Other possible

assignments include:
- a map for visitors, and related sign-system
- a school prospectus for new pupils
- the design of a completely new school.

Worked example, Key Stage 3 (Levels 3 to 7)

Schoolscapes (See Pages 30-1 of *Introducing Design*)

Context: School

Timescale: Approx. 18 hours – 9 two-hour afternoon sessions

Outcome: Artefact, system or environment to be identified by pupil or selected from a number of alternatives given.

Co-ordination: The project was run by art, CDT, English, home economics and business studies teachers.

Summary: Pupils began by making a general investigative study of their school-grounds. In choosing a suitable task those at levels 4 and 5 tended to rely on the suggestions presented in the text, whereas those at levels 6 and 7 were able to identify and negotiate their own tasks. A few pupils at level 3 needed to be set specific activities. At the conclusion of the project all pupils identified the different areas they had covered across their project as a whole. With close reference to their previous work their tutor had ensured that all pupils had extended either the breadth or depth of their knowledge, and their experience and awareness of the issues involved. On several occasions it was possible to make direct reference to topics being covered in other foundation subjects. Subsequent project work provided opportunities for more focussed activities as well as contrasting broadly-based starting points.

Pupils regularly reviewed the progress of their project and the effectiveness of their methodologies, particularly at the end of the study and design development stages. Within the time constraints of the sculpture project the models were placed against a graphic representation of their intended location and then displayed with opportunities for other members of the school to write their comments on them. A group discussion and negotiated evaluation session was held. The event which took place was judged in relation to the number who attended, the covering of the costs and the enjoyment of the participants.

The following is a selection of the range of activity which was observed and recorded at various levels across the year-group from those who chose to undertake the more open-ended Schoolscape Event or the more defined Schoolscape Sculpture.

Developing and using systems
- Some of the sculptures were kinetic and pupils explored ways of harnessing wind power and compared their findings with the advantages and disadvantages of using electric motors. They also undertook experiments using construction-kits to determine necessary changes of direction of motion and gearing.
- Two pupils took responsibility for arranging the sequence of activities on the day of the festival, and worked out where and when various activities and events would take place. A programme presenting the order, timing and location of events was produced.
- The reality of the chosen date for the event to take place on helped motivate pupils to work to the schedules they had established for themselves. These

frequently needed modification as unexpected delays, or advantageous circumstances, arose. Many pupils were working in small groups which necessitated co-ordination and co-operation.

Working with materials
- Those making sculptures undertook a series of tests to investigate the durability of possible materials under different weather conditions. Others, designing special food to sell at the event, selected and evaluated ingredients for taste, appearance and freshness.
- Students making costumes and banners for the event developed skills in the use of hand stitching and using a sewing machine.
- Skills in a wide range of realisation media and materials were developed including techniques in graphics (posters), performance (songs, music and drama), food preparation and in the sculpture project, 3D construction.

Developing and communicating ideas
- At the start of the project considerable emphasis was placed on the making, documentation and presentation of a systematic and broadly-based study of the way in which the school grounds were used and how different people thought and felt about them. Those undertaking the sculpture project visited a nearby art gallery and the workshop of a practising sculptor.
- Brainstorming techniques were widely used to generate initial ideas for themes for sculptures and the event. Where appropriate 'Theme Sheets' were prepared as a source of visual and verbal reference material. All pupils were required to produce notes and sketches as evidence that they had considered a range of possibilities for their individual projects.
- A wide variety of 2D and 3D modelling techniques were used in the development of ideas. Those designing a sculpture were advised to make an initial series of simple 3D models from card to reveal structural problems. Plan drawings, with movable card 'stalls', were used to establish the best layout and to facilitate discussion and agreement amongst the participants.
- Those making sculptures made a particular point of considering and developing the tactile and sound qualities of the materials they were using. Pupils organising the procession and dance routine were involved in creating dynamic and colourful visual and spatial effects.

Satisfying human needs
- During the initial study the purpose and value of school grounds was discussed. Some pupils made comparative studies of playgrounds in inner-city and countryside locations, and investigated common and unique games played by children from different cultural backgrounds. This research provided considerable stimulus for ideas during the project development stages.
- Those planning the event had to establish what their initial costs would be and approach various organisations to ask for funding in return for publicity. Local advertising was organised, involving posters and a publicity stunt in the centre of town the previous weekend.
- Safety considerations were important for a sculpture to be sited in a public place, uninflammable materials had to be used for costumes, and food products needed to be freshly made and presented hygienically. The pupils decided not to sell sweets and cans of drink.

Planning your own city (page 33)
City Centre Community and Local Issues provide good preparatory activities for this assignment, which could be done in as little as an hour, or extended into a long-term project in which all the main 'survival' headings are explored in detail. An alternative site and/or reason for growth, real or imaginary, which is more appropriate to the local environment of the school could be substituted. Although perhaps not essential, role-play should be encouraged as much as

possible with pupils taking individual responsibility for housing, transport, etc. An increasing population growth over the timescale of the project can provide much stimulus for identifying problems and proposals for consequent change. A small-scale city-centre model (possibly the size of a complete classroom) can be constructed in sections by pupils and used both as a 3D modelling tool and a means of final presentation.

In a co-ordinated programme of study, commencing with **Shipwrecked** and culminating in **Moonbase 2020**, this assignment could form an effective mid-point in the course.

Sources of information

The Design Council
28 Haymarket
London SW1Y 2SU (071-839 8000)

The Design Museum
Butlers Wharf
28 Shad Street
London SE1 2YD (071-403 6933)

The Engineering Council
Canberra House
10-16 Maltravers Street
London WC2R 3ER

The Science Museum
Exhibition Road
South Kensington
London

Bibliography

Objects of Desire
Forty, A
Thames and Hudson, 1986

Conran Directory of Design
Bayley, S (Ed)
Conran Octopus, 1985

Design Source Book
Sparke, Hodges, Dent-Coad and Stone
Macdonald Orbis, 1986

An Introduction to Design
Design: Processes and Products
(Unit 1, T263)
Walker, D
The Open University, 1983

Design; The Man-made Object
(T100 Units 33-4)
Walker, D
The Open University, 1978

Order in Space
Critchlow, K
Thames and Hudson, 1969

Everyday objects (page 34)

The study of existing everyday objects – familiar three-dimensional products – provides a good source for project work in which children increase their awareness about the way in which things work and how they are made. Mechanical and electronic energy and control systems can be observed in action, and production processes intelligently guessed at. The concepts of evolutionary product development, fashion and built-in obsolescence (the use of components deliberately intended to wear out after a certain length of time) are suitably introduced. Objective and subjective evaluation tests can be undertaken to assess 'fitness for purpose' and aesthetic qualities.

Asking children to re-design everyday mass-produced objects can be unrewarding, particularly if they feel they are trying to compete with professional product designers and sophisticated industrial techniques. One way to approach such activities is to ask them to design for a specific, unique situation – for a particular person or space perhaps. Using scrap materials often produces imaginative results, whilst another possibility is a multi-functional device, or to put the intended product into an entirely new context where there are no established products to mimic, such as the future, or for use on a distant planet by a life-form with some unusual characteristic, such as three arms, or 360-degree vision.

The term 'ergonomics' describes studies which relate scientifically observable information about the physical capabilities and psychological behaviour of people to the design of products, places, communications and systems. 'Anthropometrics' is specifically concerned with measurements of human size, strength and physical capacity.

Professional product designers need to take into account the fact that their products do not exist in isolation, but are components of a larger system. Artefacts not only have to work well, but have to satisfy people's psychological needs. So designers don't just design products – they are responsible for shaping the physical and emotional experiences of using them.

Human factors (page 35)
Empathy – the ability to be able to imagine how another person might think or feel – is central to the design of successful products, places and communications. Asking pupils to empathise with familiar objects is a good developmental exercise.

Product evaluation (page 36)
Ideally pupils will use the starting questions more as a checklist, and should be discouraged from providing answers which would be meaningless to someone who has not seen the list of questions. Remind pupils to refer back to the word list on page 8. The chosen product should be a real and specific item, preferably chosen by the child, and which can be seen and handled. The

Everyday Objects
Design: Processes and Products
(T263 Units 2-4)
Brown, S
The Open University, 1983

General Catalogue
Wilson, A
The Science Museum, 1988

Launch Pad Catalogue
Wilson, A
The Science Museum, 1986

household 'product' list generated on page 27 of *Introducing Design* might be a helpful starting point: generally simple objects are preferable – describing in simple terms how, for example, a computer or sewing machine actually works is not easy.

The use of particular drawing systems (e.g. orthographic or isometric) can be specified, but is perhaps best left to the child to select as appropriate. The last two questions, evaluating the way the product looks and considering if it represents value for money, are difficult, and pupils often need discussion and guidance if they are to respond with more than 'yes' or 'no' answers.

Nice and nasty (page 37)

This assignment emphasises the role of aesthetic response to texture in product design. It is also effective in getting pupils to explore and manipulate a wide range of materials, and extending critical vocabulary beyond just 'nice' and 'nasty'. Further information about polyhedral shapes will need to be provided, and pupils will quickly discover that accuracy is essential if the various faces are to end up matching together.

Everyday objectivity (page 39)

Pupils find the terms 'objective' (i.e. measurable), and 'subjective' difficult to grasp, but they can still be introduced as concepts through the process of undertaking structured testing exercises which can be numerically valued alongside those which are purely matters of opinion. They can be asked to invent ways of presenting subjective data in a more objective manner. Evaluating the effectiveness of the evaluation methods, by questioning the limitations and reliability of the information which has been discovered, is also important.

Which consumer magazine reports provide an obvious parallel and model for this assignment, though aesthetic and social design requirements, for things such as appearance and status values, also need to be fully considered. As well as evaluation from the point of view of the user, pupils should be invited to speculate as to the differing criteria and priorities the designer, the manufacturer, the factory worker, the retailer, etc., might use to assess the success of the final product.

A museum of design (page 40)

Older pupils might be able to focus on a particular product or period, and use a wide variety of primary- and secondary-source information-gathering techniques, particularly if there is a local flavour to the chosen theme. This could lead to the development of a lively exhibition using a diverse mixture of 2D and 3D presentation techniques.

Hidden uses (page 42)

Pupils are unlikely to find difficulty in identifying the various primary and secondary functions of familiar objects, but may well find the concept of tertiary functions more demanding to grasp: a good test here is to ask whether the suggested use is 'physical' – if it is then it is unlikely to be a tertiary function. A careful choice of product is important, as some have very few secondary or tertiary uses.

Final presentation sheets need to be carefully planned and developed, and checked to ensure that they are completely self-explanatory. Some children will claim not to be able to draw figures, but can be reassured that, provided the proportions are considered, simple stick or pin men will be quite adequate to communicate the intended action.

Fair exchange (page 44)

Just as there is good and bad product and architectural design, both of which we are often critical of, so there is good and bad marketing and advertising. The best genuinely helps needed products and services to become available and accessible at a reasonable price, whilst the worst persuades people to aspire to and purchase things they don't really want. Children need to become more aware of the demands and potential of sophisticated market presentation, and an increased ability to distinguish between the practical realities and their lifestyle dreams of the goods which are being offered.

The world of marketing provides a rich model for design-based assignments, particularly as the profession is already considerably 'de-signed': the term 'products' is used to refer to anything which could be goods or services, and marketing strategies involve economic and retailing decisions alongside the selection of advertising media. Marketing organisations have also developed a comprehensive and effective range of information gathering and testing techniques. These days markets are segmented not so much into A, B, C, D, and E divisions based on purchasing power and social status, but into a wide variety of lifestyle groups, such as strivers, achievers, reformers, belongers, drifters, etc., all based on our attitudes, aspirations and values. Often more time and money is spent on marketing and advertising than the design of the product or service, and agencies are diversifying into legal services and political lobbying organisations in order to manipulate potential markets.

Children may find it difficult to compete with the sophisticated levels of professionally finished artwork, but providing research and development stages have been well covered this should not prevent projects being successful. Assignments need to be related to products which children are interested in, and should be locally relevant as far as possible. Although most marketing and advertising is done by specialist consultants, some local businesses may have their own permanent departments and may be willing to become involved with local schools, and to provide good case study material.

Listening in (page 47)
The investigation phase of this assignment is a simplified version of the range of activities a company might undertake in order to discover a potential gap in an existing market. The method of preparation and presentation of a questionnaire on page 49 could be used as a reference for other assignments in the book.

Modern plastics and microchip technologies have given much greater freedom to the product designer in creating unusual forms, textures and colours which can help give an artefact a more individual and easily recognisable identity. Although an increased awareness of modern components and production methods is desirable (possibly by examining broken and unwanted radios and cassette recorders), it is not appropriate in this assignment for pupils to make working units. Instead they should concentrate on the problems of producing realistic appearance models. Wood or foam blocks usually form the best body, with other components made mainly from wood, metal and plastic off-cuts. A little rub-down instant lettering applied carefully can make a great deal of difference – it is often the quality of the final detailing which makes the model look convincing.

The assignment could be extended further by devising an advertising campaign, the production of a sales brochure, and/or an instruction leaflet, possibly in more than one language.

Soap opera (page 52)
Successful marketing involves a careful blend of decisions about the Product

Sources of further information

The Business Design Centre
52 Upper Street
Islington Green
London N1 (071-288 6480)

The Institute of Marketing
Moor Hall
Cookham
Maidenhead SL6 9QH

The Advertising Standards Authority
15/17 Ridgmount Street
London WC1E 7AW

Bibliography

Making Sense of Marketing
Robinson, G
Macmillan, 1986

The Marketing Handbook, Ch 4
Druce and Carter
NEC, 1988

Marketing Management
Kotler, P
Prentice Hall International, 1976

The Complete Guide to Advertising
Douglas, T
Macmillan, 1984

Introducing Media Studies
Series, with various titles and authors
Hodder and Stoughton, 1988/9

Other related assignments

Design, make, advertise and sell a product for a school open evening or summer fête, etc.

Devise and conduct a market research programme into domestic torches or bicycle accessories, and prepare designs for a proposed new product.

Back to nature (p. 100)
A campaign of action (p. 108)

being offered, the Place it is to be sold, the Price it will be sold at, and the way in which it will be Promoted. These are often referred to as the four P's of marketing (see page 44), and each will need to be discussed in this project, as well as how to convince the directorial board.

The seven recommendations which have to be made should not be decided upon separately, but together as part of a complete package. It is common practice to develop fully ideas for several possible brand names and images, leaving the final decision until the last moment, often in response to early market trials. Particular attention will need to be paid to the accuracy of brand names and advertising copy to ensure that they are not actually misleading.

The visual identity and promotion strategy will probably take the longest to plan and present. Pupils should be reminded of the description on page 46 of how advertisements work, and that visual images have greater impact if they are colourful, dynamic, humorous, puzzling and/or use repeated patterns. A 'unique selling proposition' (what physical and psychological benefits does this particular product offer which make it unique?) needs to be established. Most of the decisions will be found to be fairly straightforward, though it is important to emphasise that each team must present sound reasons to the directors for each of their conclusions.

The project can be reasonably covered in about two hours, but is more effective if spread over a longer time-span, allowing for more generation and evaluation of possibilities, and a more professional presentation. A 'role-play' board meeting, in which each team formally presents its ideas to the characters illustrated on the page, can make a highly effective conclusion.

Work, rest and play (page 53)

There are two distinct, yet related parts to this theme. The first is concerned with the world of work – industry and commerce – and the second with the world of leisure – what people do when they are not at work. The dividing line between the two is, of course, debatable: some individuals obtain satisfaction and relaxation from what others consider to be 'work' – physical and mental activities carried out in order to provide for human needs. Automation, changing patterns in the number of school-leavers on the market, and the consequent need to recruit skilled and semi-skilled staff willing and able to accept rapid change has led many companies towards a more enlightened view, and to recognise that their work-force often has potential which can be nurtured, valued and utilised.

As the introductory text explains, our attitudes towards play are extremely important as well. Play is a great deal more than filling time or as a relaxation and distraction from serious work. Just as young children learn skills of problem solving, language manipulation, improvisation and of codes of social behaviour, so older children and adults can benefit from understanding more about, and continuing to indulge in, play activities. And indeed it is play and leisure – sport, film and television, the arts, travel and tourism, etc. – which seem likely to become one of the major industries of the late twentieth century, particularly with increasing numbers of retired people.

Most schools already have some links with industry which could be utilised, and liaison with local primary schools for evaluation of some of the 'toy and game' projects could be well worthwhile.

Job centre (page 54)

There is growing evidence to suggest that in certain areas of the labour market,

Sources of further information

The Royal Society of Arts
John Adam Street
London WC2N 6EZ

Society of Industrial Artists and Designers
12 Carlton House Terrace
London SW1Y 5AH

Careers Research and Advisory Centre
Bateman Street
Cambridge CB2 1LZ

Young Enterprise
Robert Hyde House
48 Bryanston Square
London W1H 7LN (071-723 4070)

SATRO
1 Birdcage Walk
London SW1H 9JJ (071-222 7899)

*School/Industry Links:
A Directory of Organisations*
DES, 1986

Bibliography

Creativity and Industry
Whitfield, P
Penguin, 1975

The Biology of Work
Edholm, O
Weidenfeld and Nicholson, 1967

The Robot Book
Pawson, R
Winward, 1985

Production Systems Modelling and The Production Environment
(Units 28 and 29, T100),
Jones and Peters
The Open University, 1972

Play with a Purpose for Under-Sevens
Matterson, E M
Penguin, 1965

Learning through Play
Marzollo and Lloyd
Penguin, 1977

The Art of Lego
Exhibition Catalogue
Clwyd County Council, 1988

key staff are starting to expect rather more from their employers than just good pay and perks. A recent survey identified the following factors as being amongst the most important in the successful recruitment and retention of staff:

- a job training, career development and further education package
- a health care scheme
- recognition for contribution
- clearly defined expectations
- the opportunity to be innovative
- the general public image and status of the company.

In the mid 1990s, with the low birth-rate figure moving into the employment market, 'staff benefits' are increasingly likely to feature as part of recruitment packages. Pupils will need to be able to understand and evaluate the relative values of short- and long-term benefits and inducements. Appropriate, well-organised letters of application will remain essential, however, but it is the interview which is the critical interface in the matching of employer and employee. As a procedure, interviews are frequently a very poor method of information exchange and skill- and personality-matching. To be effective they need to be handled by a skilled interviewer and be part of a broader selection process. Prospective interviewees need to be well-prepared for such sessions, both in terms of being able to assess for themselves the appropriateness to them of the job being considered, and in communicating the necessary attitudes and abilities to the prospective employer.

The domestic help (page 55)
This assignment is essentially about the way in which people respond to ideas about the anticipated quality of life in an automated, de-personalised society. Household humanoid robots are, of course, still a long way off, but we already rely on many 'labour-saving' devices – until they go wrong and we discover we can't repair them. Then we soon begin to feel deprived and frustrated, aggravated and alienated when we are unable to obtain a personal response from the large security-conscious, cost-effective, multi-conglomerate manufacturers who don't offer a proper locally-based maintenance service.

Cartoon sequences have much to offer as a communication exercise, though as an alternative pupils could make collages, construct 3D models, and/or drama sequences based on the poem, constructing appropriate costumes and props.

Robomotion (page 56)
The technical term which describes the mimicking of human movements by machines is 'prosthetics'. This project will help reveal the subtleties and sophistication of human actions we take for granted, and the considerable problems of trying to imitate them mechanically. A variation would be to look at animal or insect movements. Although the initial analysis of the sequence of movement is fairly easy, reference to biology textbooks is likely to be needed to establish more exactly what is happening under the skin: some awareness of basic mechanisms and control systems is also needed. Initially pupils might, for comparison, try constructing prototypes made exclusively from technical construction kits or from traditional construction materials, and then be encouraged to mix the two as appropriate in a final construction.

Fun machines (page 58)
Ideally children will choose their own possible sites, but it might be preferred to pre-select a specific local site which a class could all visit and study together. At the centre of this assignment is the transformation of the thematic images into play or fairground type structures – a process which many pupils will find initially difficult – and some further illustrative examples may be needed. The project could be extended through the analysis of the mechanical properties and energy systems of traditional playground equipment and modern theme-park rides, and the construction of working models of ideas. Taken even further,

the design of an entire theme park is a good basis for an extended cross-curricular activity, covering most of the basic technological headings.

Joyful noises (page 59)

In this assignment it is important for pupils to be aware of the different ways in which young children play with toys during the various stages of their development. Ideally this might come from first-hand observation at local playgroups or primary schools, or from watching young brothers or sisters: this should be supported by an analysis of existing toys on the market. Designing for handicapped or disabled children can be an effective variation.

The 'sound' element in the activity provides a useful experimental starting point, and also helps children to move away from simple direct copies of existing designs: the noises could of course be mechanically or electronically generated. The final end-product does not strictly need to be pull-along, particularly if a less constructionally complex approach is sought, and could be more in the form of a learning-aid or game.

Fun and games (page 60)

This assignment frequently has a high success rate, but does need to be properly researched and developed by pupils if the results are to exploit fully its educational potential. What makes many board-games 'fun' for most children is their role-play dimension, and unless the visual images and associated words are strong enough they are unlikely to be effective. The prototyping stage is also important as it provides an excellent opportunity for pupils to undertake (and very much enjoy!) a rapid make/test/evaluate/modify/re-test sequence.

As with many everyday products, the 'instructions for use', are extremely important and need to be carefully considered. First attempts usually produce an over-long written description, and pupils need to be encouraged to analyse and provide the essential information and to use visually-based instructions wherever possible. Production-line costing and visually-related packaging, marketing and advertising are further considerations to extend the scope of the assignment.

Sources of further information

Royal Institute of British Architects
66 Portland Place
London W1N 4AD (071-580 5533)

Bibliography

Architecture for Beginners
Hellman, L
Unwin, 1986

Shelter (page 62)

Shelter is a theme with many possibilities and dimensions, providing a good mixture of human physical and psychological needs and technical constraints and possibilities which relate together materials, structures and energy systems. Although contemporary western houses are quick to build and often cheap to run, they are often inflexible, spatially weak and have inadequate circulation space, storage facilities and levels of natural light. All children at some stage in their lives are likely to have to make decisions about the shelter they will live in, and need to be able to recognise well-designed interiors that are both efficient and friendly, and that they can adapt to suit their changing requirements.

Most subjects will be able to contribute to this theme, and projects tend to cover the full range of design skills. In *Introducing Design* an extended series of short-term activities has been utilised, based on one central design activity. Other related projects could, however, work in a variety of different ways. Liaison with county council planning offices, local architectural practices and urban study centres is likely to be well worthwhile.

My house (page 64)

These introductory activities involve pupils in making a study of their existing houses and increase their familiarity with some of the main conventions of architectural drawings. They make a good direct follow-on from the **Products,**

Spacecraft, Ch. 4
Ball, R
George Philips, 1987

Home, Living With Technology
(T101 Unit 1)
Cross and Steadman
The Open University, 1979

Houses: analysis and synthesis
Design; Processes and Products
(T263 Units 8-10)
Vale B and R
The Open University, 1983

Places and Communications text and assignments on pages 26 and 27.

About 15 minutes needs to be allowed for the memory drawing in **What does your house look like?**, which introduces the concept of a two-dimensional elevation. The most common mistakes are likely to be misjudging the height of the roof, and not aligning ground and first floor doors and windows. Pupils who live in flats could attempt to draw the main entrance area, or a communal corridor: a relative or friend's house is another alternative.

The house-interviewing activity in **How does your house work?** extends the idea of empathy. Pupils will need to be encouraged to develop imaginative responses, and can be invited to suggest further appropriate questions. An initial rough version should proceed a final presentation. As an alternative, pupils could interview each other's houses, their classrooms or familiar public buildings. Another possibility is to set up a 'chat-show' format, with responses being made verbally (and dramatically), rather than graphically.

Ideally the rough ground and first floor house plans should be positioned side-by side. Most pupils will find getting the correct proportions of passageways, doors and furniture difficult, and careful checking at home is important. As well as introducing the idea of the plan drawing, other architectural drawing conventions (e.g. for windows and doorways), and measured scales can be covered in the final, neat version.

Following the plan, a symbolic representation can be developed in **A functional diagram of your house**. Pupils often find initial difficulty in translating the layout and scale of the spaces into simple circles and lines. The final diagram is important for a later activity in **All change**. Once the concept of the plan and elevation has been grasped, pupils should be able to construct simple axonometric drawings, providing they remember to follow the basic sequence of instructions. Common mistakes include forgetting to start by drawing the plan tilted through 45 degrees, and not checking that all lines which are vertical in reality are vertical on the drawing.

All change (page 67)
The first activity in this assignment is intended to be imaginative, in contrast to the considerable constraints which are subsequently applied. As well as their own dreams, pupils should be encouraged to take into account the aspirations of other members of their family as well. The later development of ideas follows on from the **Functional Diagram** activity on page 66, or could be based on the information matrix and net procedure presented on pages 82 and 83.

As well as plan representations of proposed rooms and corridors, pupils should be encouraged to use sketch elevations and axonometrics and simple card scale models to assist them in the development of their ideas. Ideally they should be able to imagine themselves in the spaces they are creating, moving round from room to room. Where difficulties are found perceiving the spaces full-size, then full-size tape-drawings of room plans and/or elevations can be very effectively used, if space permits. Common errors are to make corridors too long, dark and narrow, to make doorways too small, or not to leave enough space to be able to move easily around the furniture: a comparison of the preparatory and final plan drawings on page 70 shows how such problems need to be tackled. Pupils should be allowed to break the 'rules' which are given, but only if they can convincingly justify the increased cost of doing so in terms of the overall benefits which would be achieved.

The project might be extended in a number of ways. The outside of the structure could be considered in much more detail, including the possible roof-pitch structures, the building materials and facings to external walls. Doors and windows could be precisely specified, and the whole structure could be costed.

Designing the front and/or back garden area is another possibility.

Where final models have been made they can be used for the final **On site** part of the project, although the activity can also be done as an A3 or A4 paper exercise. This activity could be tackled in very much greater depth with visits being made to contrasting local housing estates, and a town planner invited in to talk to the group. Further detailing could be included with the design and placing of road lights, litter-bins and street signs, and finding out more about regulations regarding access for fire and refuse services. Another variation would be to base the exercise on a real local site. The **Community** theme provides a particularly appropriate follow-on at this point.

Sources of further information

The Design Council
28 Haymarket
London SW1Y 2SU (071-839 8000)

The Design Museum
Butlers Wharf
28 Shad Street
London SE1 2YD (071-403 6933)

Bibliography

Television Graphics
Merritt, D
Trefoil, 1987

How to Design Trademarks and Logos
Murphy and Rowe
Phaidon, 1988

Graphic Design Source Book
McQuiston and Kitts
Macdonald Orbis, 1987

Mind Over Matter
Pedler, K
Thames Methuen, 1981

Museum of the Moving Image,
Catalogue
British Film Institute, 1988

Information (page 72)

The information technology revolution has only just begun. During the next twenty or so years the speed of access to database systems and global communication networks will make an impact on the nature and quality of our everyday lives which is difficult to imagine or predict. The implications for the ways of work, the exchange of goods, financial services, entertainment and education are considerable. Interactive video-technology, linked to sophisticated computer systems will radically transform the way we transmit, store, retrieve and perceive symbolic, verbal and visual information. Indeed it has been suggested that 85 per cent of information is now received optically, so children need to be able to be visually, as well as verbally and mathematically, literate.

The processes of design and technological education provide an excellent opportunity for the growth of pupils' capability in the practical use of information technology systems. In terms of problem-investigation an increasing amount of verbal and visual information is now available on computer and video databases which can be rapidly identified, accessed and cross-referenced from across the world if necessary. A computer can also effectively be used in the construction and controlled manipulation of models. As well as verbal and numerical experiments and predictions, visual images can often be generated more quickly and accurately than conventional techniques permit. All stages of the evolution of a model can be recorded for later reference. Computer- and video-generated images have proved to be very dynamic forms of public visual communication, and are already extensively used commercially. Local cable networks will, however, enable anyone to communicate using such systems – perhaps even to advertise a forthcoming school concert or fête. The potential impact of desk-top publishing is still difficult to assess at this stage, but it seems likely that an increasing number of non-specialists will become responsible for specifying typographic design and layout. Meanwhile in the production industries, detailed specifications and drawings can now be passed directly to automated machines.

Most important though is the development of an awareness of when it is more appropriate to use a graphics-tablet and a spread-sheet, and when the time has come to switch off the technology and go out to make more personal contact.

Seen in these ways, opportunities to develop information technology awareness and capability are to be found throughout the assignments of *Introducing Design*. The theme as a whole is **not** therefore based specifically on computer studies or discrete information technology activities, but on all areas of the curriculum involved in developing communication skills.

Communication evaluation (page 73)

Of all the three **evaluation** assignments, pupils are likely to find this is the most difficult, as they tend to be less experienced in considering graphic material than products and places. Most will manage the descriptive section, though will probably need prompting if they are to think of further relevant questions for themselves: the evaluation will almost certainly need discussion if the sophistication of much contemporary graphic work is to be perceived.

Person to person (page 74)
Some imaginative thinking, based on popular science fiction, is needed to transform everyday small-scale communication devices into something less conventional. Some simple paper or card models are useful to establish appropriate sizes and positions for controls, and to work out exactly how it will be practically 'worn'. Considerable ingenuity and workmanship is needed to make an effective final model.

Mind over matter (page 77)
Some people appear to have a 'sixth sense' – the ability to communicate ideas telepathically: such messages tend to be visual rather than verbal. Pupils should be encouraged to consider and select a variety of 2D and 3D static and dynamic images for comparison purposes. The experiment needs to be set up in as objective and scientific a manner as possible. A 'control group' could be established, and the results analysed statistically.

Communication breakdown (page 77)
This assignment is intended to develop further the ability to empathise. Presentation could be through a cartoon strip, or a short improvised drama.

Symbols and logos (page 78)
Contemporary corporate images often represent visual communication in its most sophisticated form: a simple graphic device can not only link a diverse range of products and services together, but also say a great deal about the nature and quality of the company, perhaps representing security, tradition, new technology, durability, reliability, speed and efficiency of service, etc. Perhaps the cleverest symbols of all are those which contain a puzzle. Our mind is absorbed for a few moments trying to work out why the design looks like that. And when we've worked it out we feel clever at our ability to solve the problem – a satisfaction which is renewed every time we see the symbol and transferred to our perception of the company and its products.

Pupils cannot be expected to achieve highly sophisticated levels of professional design, but the process of developing logos and symbols nevertheless provides an excellent opportunity for them to move rapidly through a structured generation, transformation and evaluation sequence. A common failing is to produce designs which are too complex. Where available, pupils can be shown the considerable value of a photocopier and a micro-computer in the design of graphic images.

As a follow-up assignment, children can be asked to design logos or symbols for imaginary companies, each concerned with different types of products and services. This could be extended to a real, local small business or charitable organisation, with the manager providing background information and a basic brief.

Transport (page 80)

We travel about every day and take it all for granted. Our lifestyles are probably shaped more than anything else by our ability to get ourselves and our belongings from one place to another. Our attitudes towards transport might need to change over the next twenty or so years however: increased speed

Sources of further information

Transport 2000 Ltd
Walkdon House
10 Melton Street
London NW1 2EJ

Department of Transport
Mersham Street
London

Docklands Light Railways Ltd
PO Box 154
Poplar
London E14 9QA (071-538 0311)

Bibliography

Bicycles: Invention and Innovation
Design; Processes and Products
(T263 Units 5-7),
Roy, R
The Open University, 1983

Cars: Forms and Futures
Design; Processes and Products
(T263 Units 11-13),
Walker, D
The Open University, 1983

The Car Programme
Bayley, S
Boilerhouse/V&A (Design Museum)

over long distances makes travel increasingly dangerous, especially where safety standards are ignored to keep costs down. In towns and cities the roadway systems are becoming more and more unable to cope efficiently with their increased use, and fuel pollutes the atmosphere and consumes natural resources at an alarming rate.

Because the 'products' of transport – vehicles, railway carriages, etc. – are extremely sophisticated and large-scale it is difficult to find suitable projects based on their design. For this reason assignments in this theme tend to concentrate more on the social implications and effects of transport, and aim to raise awareness of the relationships between cost, speed, convenience and comfort – decisions about which we take everyday in our choice of method of travel. Older students will later find a subtle mixture of technical factors and human requirements in aspects of vehicle design, for example, which involves a wide range of mechanical and electronic energy control systems, often related to aerodynamic considerations, combined with the need for ergonomically-designed controls and interiors. Marketing and advertising add a further dimension.

Although not included in *Introducing Design*, the study and design of bicycle components and accessories can be a wide-ranging and successful assignment, ranging from safety devices to lighting devices, protective clothing, styling and the local routing of bicycle lanes. The managers of local bus or train stations or other transport-related organisations may well be willing to present details of the particular problems they face.

Saver return (page 81)
The research for this assignment involves consulting maps and timetables as well as finding out about costs. Some of this information could be provided, but most pupils should not find it too difficult to obtain for themselves – particularly if they are encouraged to divide the tasks up between themselves. Getting the presentation right will need several versions, and mixtures of different techniques of verbal, visual and symbolic communication systems will need to be experimented with.

Terminus (page 82)
The starting points for this assignment will depend to a certain extent on the locality of the school and its proximity to an existing transport terminus of some sort. It is not necessary to stick to the theme of buses, and an airport, dockland or train station concourse could easily be substituted. Where there is access to a nearby facility a class study-visit would prove well worthwhile. There are many detailed problems of diverse things such as information and sign systems, litter, left-luggage, seating, etc., which pupils should easily be able to identify.

The development stage, using the matrix and net, will probably need to be carefully explained and structured by the teacher, especially with younger pupils. The final presentation could be extended by a wide range of graphic presentation techniques and models. If a team approach is used each design group and a number of outsiders could evaluate a presentation of the range of alternative schemes. A mock planning enquiry could be held, or accounts of the competing schemes documented in newspaper reports or in local TV and radio news items.

Holiday exchange (page 84)
After following the basic scenario outlined in the assignment, pupils should be invited to invent their own characters, and to introduce unexpectedly other incidences and problems which the passengers and airport staff will have to respond to.

On the run (page 85)

The basis of this assignment is the well-established CDT 'design a device to travel a certain distance' project, extended to include considerations for the passenger.

Legoids (page 86)

There is much to be discovered by looking at the way in which nature works. Although people's bodies, brains and senses are highly efficient in some respects, human beings do many things very crudely when compared to the abilities of most animals and insects: our hearing is relatively crude, our sense of taste saturated and our sense of smell minimal. And it has been suggested that we don't really believe in the senses which really matter. Engineers have discovered a great deal about balance, control, leverage, materials, and communication and navigation systems from the investigation of biological phenomena.

In this assignment an initial preparatory study (which could include a collage sheet based on 'articulation') should move rapidly into an experimental phase using 3D materials and construction kits: such experiments should of course be fully documented. The project could be extended by asking pupils to devise instruction sheets clear enough for a younger child to make an identical model, or by asking them to produce a piece of graphic work in which the perceived scale of their machine is enlarged (or diminished), by showing it in proportional relationship to people and landscape features.

Increasing speed (page 87)

The passage is based on an extract from *Future Shock* (A Toffler, 1970). Toffler uses it as an example of the current speed of the rate of change of technological capability, suggesting that human beings are quite unprepared and unable to deal with the current rate of technological change. He provides a further illustration based on the division of the past 50 000 years into 800 lifetimes of 62 years each. During the first 650 of the 800 lifetimes, human beings continued to be cave dwellers. 70 lifetimes ago writing and drawing made communication from one generation to the next possible. Printing has only been available to the past six generations, the electric motor to the past two. And, as Toffler points out, the vast majority of today's familiar products, places and communications have only been developed within the present, 800th lifetime. These figures could be used as the basis of a different or further graphic representation.

Clothing (page 88)

Sources of further information

Clothing and Footwear Institute
71 Brushfield Street
London E1 6AA (071-247 1696)

CAPITB
80 Richardshaw Lane
Pudsey
Leeds LS28 6BN (0532 393355)

The Crafts Council
8 Waterloo Place
London SW1Y 4AT (071-930 4811)

Despite the fact that this country produces some of the world's most influential fashion designers, the British public remain highly conservative in their attitude to the everyday clothes they wear. 'Fashion' is not so much associated with a high quality of design, fabrication and material, but more with superficiality and impracticability. As a result high-street multiples sell clothing which is unadventurous and limited in range, and manufacturing industries have become unwilling to move away from large-scale batch production.

The potential for our clothing to be decorative and symbolic, combined with its more functional, protective role provides a theme which potentially covers a wide range of possibilities for design and technological activity. In this way it can become divorced from the discrete images of 'needlework and dressmaking' and appeal equally to boys and girls. In an historical context, examining fashionable and protective garments reveals much of the social structures and working conditions of the day, and in the present day effectively deals with techniques of mass production, the values of the 'throw-away' society

Victoria & Albert Museum
South Kensington
London

Bibliography

Fashion Source Book
De La Haye
Macdonald Orbis, 1988

Directory of Twentieth Century Fashion
McDowell, C
Frederick Muller, 1984

Covering Up
Smart and Griffiths
Science Museum, 1982

Fashion and Surrealism
Martin, R
Thames and Hudson, 1988

The New Jewelry
Dormer and Turner
Thames and Hudson, 1985

Starting Textiles
Stables, K
Macmillan, 1988

Home Economics in Action – Textiles
Christian Carter, J
Oxford University Press, 1988

Body Styles
Polhemus, Sidgwick and Jackson, Channel 4, 1989

Other related assignments

Packing a suitcase for a particular type of journey or holiday, e.g. a mountain hike, a safari, etc.

Items of personal adornment made from scrap or low-cost materials.

Protective clothing for young children to use whilst walking to school, or riding a bike.

Face-painting, together with head-wear and other accessories.

Materials testing using a range of natural and synthetic fabrics.

and the need for compromise between style and utility. Children also need to become more aware of the way in which their clothing reveals a great deal about their tastes, personalities and attitudes.

Fit for the job (page 89)
These three activities form a useful preparation for the subsequent assignments in this section. Fifty different examples of specialist clothing are not in fact very difficult to generate, with a little bit of encouragement. Inviting an outsider into school to discuss the uniform or protective clothing they wear is effective. Discarded items of clothing could be taken to pieces to reveal the ways in which they have been shaped and joined. The **Fancy dress** could be made up at doll-/Action-Man-size rather than full-scale, and placed in an appropriate model setting.

Off the peg (page 90)
In schools where uniform is worn, this will be a topical subject which will appeal to most pupils. The assignment could be introduced with a historical study of how school uniforms have developed, utilising surviving examples and the memories of older relatives (and teachers!). The concept of some sort of uniform is frequently endorsed; it is the lack of practicality and appropriate visual appearance which tends to be found lacking in many present solutions. For the purposes of this assignment, the practicalities of manufacture of the design of a proposed uniform should be secondary to the increased awareness of the need to satisfy a wide range of opinions, the probably mixed responses to the initiation of processes of change within an institution, and the need for effectiveness in communication skills. Pupils should be reminded to refer to the **Symbols and Logos** assignment on page 79 when considering the design of a new school badge.

Roboritual (page 92)
After the general investigation stage, pupils will probably need some guidelines on basic structural approaches to the mask – how it will be made and prevented from falling off. A practical experimentation stage is extremely important to discover interesting and unusual textures and colours and the way in which scrap materials can be effectively utilised. The full costume and/or the ritual performance could be left out if preferred. Beyond the designing and making of the mask are of course important discussion issues of our present attitudes towards the advantages and disadvantages of technology.

Any colour you like/Fantastic hats (page 96)
The possibilities of a fashion show presentation at the end of these assignments should not be ignored. A simple 'cat-walk' area can be defined, and appropriate music selected. Pupils will need to rehearse their movements, and to make sure everything is properly organised back-stage to ensure fast and efficient changes of costume. If possible a video record of the event should be made.

Food (page 98)

In recent years people have become a great deal more interested in the food they consume, both in terms of quality, through 'gourmet' publications, television programmes and advertising, and in quantity – diet and the dangers of contamination. As well as developing skills of food preparation, children need to be able to take decisions about the appropriateness of what they eat and drink, and increase their awareness of the issues involved in the commercial technologies of producing and selling mass-produced food.

The activities and issues involved in this theme clearly go beyond acquiring

Bibliography

Home Economics in Action – Food
Christian Carter, J
Oxford University Press, 1986

Nuffield Home Economics
Hutchinson, 1985

Food Investigations
Wynn, B
Oxford, 1986

Food Tables
Bender and Bender
Oxford, 1986

Sources of further information

Environment Council
80 York Way
London N1 9AG

Friends of the Earth
26-28 Underwood Street
London N1 7JQ

Greenpeace
30-31 Islington Green
London N1 8XE

Centre for Alternative Technology
Llwyngwern Quarry
Machynlleth
Powys SW20 9AZ

Bibliography

The Big E
McCarry and Pollock
BBC Education 1989

basic cookery skills. Whilst home economics clearly has an important role to play in this theme there is much scope for utilising cross-curricular approaches, which is particularly necessary if it is not to be perceived as something more appropriate to girls than boys.

Back to nature (page 100)

This assignment could be undertaken on an individual basis instead of as a group activity, as described. Preparing the collage is an important initial activity in order that it can serve as a reference for later tasks: the use of a broad range of sources and imagery needs to be encouraged, and the layout and composition of the sheet will need some consideration. Identifying possible names and developing designs for the symbol will take some time to do properly: pupils should refer back to the **Symbols and Logos** assignment on page 79 and follow a similar approach, substituting possible names for the company.

In tackling the rest of the activities, pupils will need to begin with some further analysis and investigation. They need to be frequently reminded to provide clear evidence of the decision-making processes they are following. It is often worth insisting that a number of different possibilities for sites, uniforms, street frontages, etc., must be generated and evaluated before a final decision on each is taken, with the reasons very clearly stated. A possible extension of the project, if time and space permits, could be the creation of a complete full-scale restaurant environment in the corner of a classroom. Uniforms could be made up, actual food prepared and so on. Role-play situations could be set up – awkward customers, staff problems, the opening ceremony, press coverage, etc.

Design and society (page 104)

The alliance of design, technological and environmental issues emerged publicly during the early 1970s. As a result of the oil crisis, architects began to design 'energy-conscious' buildings. Product designers read Papenak's *Design for the Real World*, and talked of 'design for need' – for the handicapped and elderly. Awareness of the concepts of the need to develop sources of alternative energy, of 'self-sufficiency' and *The Good Life* was at its height in the mid-decade, but somehow was never really taken seriously by mainstream society and politicians.

By the early 1980s 'pollution' had become cliché, and style, fashion and the commercial values of obsolescence dominated product development. The summer of 1988, however, marked a fairly sudden turning-point, sparked off by the plight of the seals off the east coast of England which caught and focussed public concern. Firm evidence of damage to the ozone layer by CFCs emerged, made real to the public by a seemingly noticeable change to weather patterns, both in Europe and around the world. The destruction of the rain forests was widely featured by the Sunday newspapers, with the assurance that each edition was printed on trees specially grown for the purpose. During the autumn, all the political parties went various shades of rather artificial 'green' at their conferences, and supermarkets replaced leaflets about the nutritional values of their products with information about their ozone-friendly packaging.

As well as the promotion of lead-free petrol, a series of transport issues emerged at this time too. Motorway and town-centre congestion seemed to reach an unacceptable peak, and an unusually close series of major rail and air disasters began to raise serious questions about safety standards. Chicken- and egg-contamination stories led to an increased concern about the safety of food production methods. In contrast to the 1950s, when everyone seemed to think

The Autonomous House
Vale, B and R
Thames and Hudson, 1975

The Waste Makers
Packard, V
Penguin, 1960

Design for the Real World
Papanek, V
Thames and Hudson, 1972

Designing The Future
Unit 1, Man-made Futures (T262)
Cross, Elliot and Roy
Open University Publications, 1975

Small is Beautiful
Schumacher, E F
Abacus, 1975

What on Earth Are We Doing?
Keen and Simmons
Ladybird Books, 1976

*Nuffield Co-ordinated Science –
Physics*
*Nuffield Co-ordinated Science –
Biology*
Longman, 1988

that science and technology would solve all the problems of the world, our awareness today of the potential disadvantages of technology is considerably greater.

Recycled information (page 107)
Some bookwork will be needed to obtain some further information to form the basis of the poster. Pupils need to be reminded of some of the guidelines to the design of successful posters:
- devise strong simple visual images (colourful, dynamic, puzzling, humorous, etc.) to capture attention and to prompt action
- a good main caption is needed
- experiment with the use of different layouts of text and illustrations.

A campaign of action (page 108)
A broad and active approach to this assignment should be encouraged, with particular reference back to **Fair exchange** on page 44.

Futurehome 2000 (page 109)
Ideally pupils will have already undertaken the **My House** and **All Change** assignments from the **Shelter** section and therefore be able to apply similar developmental processes to this project. Variations of the activity include:
- designing for a specific local site
- providing a high level of self-sufficiency by including provision for growing food and keeping animals
- making a scale cut-away model as part of the final realisation
- devising and presenting a related drama sequence set in the future home.

At some stage pupils should be asked to evaluate what they consider to be the likelihood of each of their main ideas becoming reality by the turn of the century. What further technological developments, or changes in political policies and social attitudes might first be needed?

Moonbase: a giant leap for mankind (page 110)
This assignment can be effectively compared and contrasted with the introductory **Shipwrecked** projects: as such it could form an appropriate conclusion to a programme of study. Again pupils will need to use their imaginations to remove themselves from present day reality, and consider how they would approach the problems of physical and psychological survival in an isolated environment. Depending on the intended scope and time-scale of the assignment (which might range from a few sessions in which just one topic is examined, to a full-scale extended cross-curricular activity), further research could be undertaken to discover more about the environmental condition of the moon, and actual possible sites for settlement. There is also considerable scope for conclusive graphic, model-making and performance presentations.

A variation is to place the assignment in the context of an orbiting space station, or a long-distance space voyage. In all three situations an interesting comparison might be made with the present designs of large-scale shopping malls where a wide range of survival needs are provided for in a controlled environment.

Other books of general interest

Women in Design
McQuiston, L
Trefoil, 1988

*Where Things Come From and How
They Are Made*
Cook and Bond
Usborne Books. 1989

Project Proposal

Name
Form

Date

Statement of problem

Starting questions

Sources of information

Expected outcomes

Project Summary/Record

Name
Form

Task
Date

Student's summary of task

Student's evaluation

Tutors' comments

- Investigation
- First thoughts
- Developing detailed ideas
- Realisation and presentation
- Planning and organisation
- Evaluation

Project Schedule

Name
Form

Task

Date	Intended actions	Results/further action	Tutors' comments